MARINE ANIMALS OF
BAJA CALIFORNIA

A Guide to the Common Fish
and Invertebrates

by

Daniel W. Gotshall

SEA CHALLENGERS
LOS OSOS, CALIFORNIA   ●   **WESTERN MARINE ENTERPRISES**
VENTURA, CALIFORNIA

A SEA CHALLENGERS AND
WESTERN MARINE ENTERPRISES PUBLICATION

FRONT COVER

Clarion angelfish, *Holacanthus clarionensis*, upper right
Gulf star, *Oreaster occidentalis*, lower left

Photographs Daniel W. Gotshall

ISBN: 0-930036-24-9 (Paperbound)
ISBN: 0-9300118-08-1 (Hardcover)

Library of Congress Catalog Card Number: 82-050492

SEA CHALLENGERS
1851 DON AVENUE
LOS OSOS, CALIFORNIA 93402

WESTERN MARINE ENTERPRISES
P.O. BOX Q
VENTURA, CALIFORNIA 93002

Printed by Dai Nippon Printing Co., Ltd., Tokyo, Japan.

Phototypesetting and pre-press production by Padre Productions, San Luis Obispo, CA

DEDICATION

This book is dedicated to John Fitch, naturalist and ichthyologist, whose guidance, support, and friendship have been of inestimable value to me, whose dedication to the highest ideals of scientific endeavor has been a constant inspiration to all fortunate enough to know him, and whose example and advice initially led me to the task of collecting photographs and writing about Pacific Coast fishes and invertebrates.

TABLE OF CONTENTS

INTRODUCTION

Marine Animals of Baja California describes 125 species of fishes and 62 species of invertebrates that are commonly encountered in the shallow waters surrounding the Baja California peninsula. The photographs of live fishes and invertebrates were obtained on a series of expeditions along the outer peninsula coast, within the Sea of Cortez, and as far as 250 miles S.W. of Cabo San Lucas to the Islas Revillagigedos.

As with my previous books, this field guide is designed to be used by snorkelers, sport divers, naturalists, and professional biologists — in short, anyone interested in diving and exploring the shallow waters of this unique region and who wishes to learn more about its marine life.

To the best of my knowledge, this field guide is the first all-color photo guide to both the fishes and invertebrates of the area. Two previously published books, *The Reef Fishes of the Sea of Cortez* (Thompson, et al.) and *Gulf of California Fishwatcher's Guide* (Thompson and McKibbin) specifically cover the fishes of the entire Gulf of California. The former, which includes up-to-date life history information for many of the species, was the first book to catalogue and describe the fishes that spend most of their lives in, on, or around reefs. The latter book is a field guide, utilizing line drawings to describe the more common Gulf fishes most likely to be encountered by fishermen, divers, and snorkelers. Both of these books were invaluable in helping me to identify the fishes I encountered on my diving/photo expeditions.

At this time, there is only one book available that deals with Gulf of California invertebrates — *Common Intertidal Invertebrates of the Gulf of California* by Brusca. This reference uses narrative descriptions and keys to describe the animals, but, unfortunately, contains only a few drawings and photographs. It nevertheless has proved quite useful to me in identifying many of the invertebrates I encountered and photographed. For more information on these references, please consult the bibliography on page 110.

I have excluded most of the fishes and invertebrates whose southern range extends down the outer coast of Baja from California, since these animals are included in *Pacific Coast Inshore Fishes* (Gotshall) and *Pacific Coast Subtidal Marine Invertebrates* (Gotshall and Laurent). These animals are common around both San Benitos Islands and Cedros Islands. If you are planning a trip to either of these areas, you will need all three books.

I have also excluded most of the small fishes such as gobies, tube blennies, and clingfish that are almost impossible to identify underwater or tend to spend most of their lives hidden away from the diver's view. The invertebrate section, which begins on page 76, contains only the most common species that divers are likely to see; I have excluded invertebrates that can only be found by digging in the sand or mud or by turning over rocks. I have also excluded most of the molluscs as these are covered quite well in other books (see bibliography). The photographs do include many of the fish and invertebrates that live on the shallow, sandy bottoms and many of the large, pelagic jacks that are so abundant around the Islas Revillagigedos.

As with my other books, rather than long narrative descriptions, I have stressed the use of color plates and keys to identify the fish and invertebrates. For each species illustrated, in addition to maximum known size, habitat, and known geographic range, I have provided one or two identifying characters to look for underwater.

An asterisk * identifies information that has not previously been published. In some cases another species is mentioned in the description but is not illustrated; these are indicated by (NI). The identifications in this guide, to the very best of my knowledge, are correct; however, because the taxonomy of the marine animals of this region has not received much attention in the past, some of the scientific names could prove to be in error in the future, as more detailed studies are completed. This is particularly true of the invertebrates. You will note that I have identified many of the invertebrates only as far as genus, either because the species has not yet been described, or because information is still lacking as to which species it might be. Although several taxonomists have looked at the invertebrate photographs and either confirmed or corrected my identifications on specific organisms, I alone am responsible for the final choice of names used for the animals. Of particular difficulty were the very rich assemblages of Gulf gorgonions; thus, I frankly admit that some of these creatures may not have the correct scientific name. Should the reader be aware of any errors in identification, or know of additional information, such as new range extensions or sizes, I would very much appreciate hearing from you so that corrections can be included in future printings.

NOMENCLATURE: The common English and Spanish names of the fishes are those used in *The Reef Fishes of the Sea of Cortez*. Common names of invertebrates, although it is highly upsetting to some scientists, are in most cases of my own coinage and are for descriptive purposes only.

Scientific names of fishes are taken from either *The Reef Fishes of the Sea of Cortez* or other recent scientific literature. Invertebrate scientific names are either from *Common Intertidal Invertebrates of the Gulf of California* or those supplied by taxonomists (see acknowledgements).

HOW TO USE FIELD GUIDES: The best way of learning to identify any plant or animal is to make it a habit of leafing through your field guide and reviewing the photographs before going into the field. This practice I find partiulary useful prior to a dive so that the photographs will be fresh in my mind. I think you will find that with this constant reviewing, the shapes and colors of the animals or plants quickly become very familiar. You may not remember the name immediately, but you will be able to go back to the field guide later and readily locate the organism.

When using this guide, should the animal be completely unfamiliar, turn to the pictorial keys on pages 9 & 76 and find the fish or invertebrate that most closely resembles the animal you observed in shape and other characteristics. Then turn to the page listed for that family and look at the photographs; more than likely your fish or invertebrate will be easily recognizable.

NEW INFORMATION: Despite a great deal of work that has been done on classifying and describing the fish and invertebrates of the Gulf of California, the surface has barely been scratched, and it will require many more years of dedicated work both by scientists and non-scientists to reach the status of our current knowledge of the fish and invertebrates of the Pacific Coast inshore waters north of Mexico.

My primary reason for producing this guide is to help increase knowledge and awareness about the marine animals of the Gulf. You, the reader, can help by providing me or other interested researchers with your own observations on new geographic range, depth range, or life history information. I would like, therefore, to encourage you to write to me with any such information or corrections you might have. Please address your comments to the author at SEA CHALLENGERS, 1851 Don Avenue, Los Osos, California 93402.

ACKNOWLEDGMENTS

This book could not have been written without the assistance of the following individuals: Kenneth Hashagen, California Department of Fish and Game, served as general editor of the manuscript and galleys; Robert N. Lea, California Department of Fish and Game, and Richard Brusca, University of Southern California, served as technical editors for fishes and invertebrates respectively. Kirk M. Stoddard, Interstate Electronics, and Lilliam Dempster, California Academy of Sciences, translated the scientific names of the invertebrates and fishes respectively. Confirmations of and identifications of species were made by John McCosker and John Hewitt, Steinhart Aquarium, Dustin Chivers and Staff, California Academy of Sciences, Ronald Mc Peak, Kelco Co., Eric Hochberg, Santa Barbara Museum of Natural History, David W. Behrens, Pacific Gas and Electric Co., Robert Given, University of Southern California, Marine Science Center, Santa Catalina Island, Robert N. Lea, Hans Bertsch, Universidad Autonoma de Baja California, Mexico, John E. Fitch and John D. McEachran, Texas A & M University.

Sandy Dostalek, Betty Herold and Ann Gotshall typed the manuscript. Expeditions were conducted aboard the La Paz based *Baja Explorador* jointly owned by Ted and Lois Ann Waltham and Oscar and Elena Moreno.

To all of these people, to the crew of the *Baja Explorador*, the many expedition co-participants, and to anyone I may have inadvertently overlooked, I owe a great debt of gratitude.

PHOTO AND ART CREDITS

Photographer	Species Number
Greg Aeschliman	84, 97 (fishes)
David Behrens	7, 8, 12, 28, 29, 52, 54 (invertebrates)
Jack Dodd	2, 29 b (fishes) 35 (invertebrates)
Robert Given	13d (invertebrates)
Alex Kerstitch	21, 60, 107 (fishes)
Laurence Laurent	22 (fishes)
Jim Mattison Jr.	25 (fishes)
Flip Nicklin, Nicklin and Associates	1 (fishes)
Dan Odenweller	114 (fishes)
Tom Wilson	62 (invertebrates)

All other photographs by Daniel Gotshall.

Drawings of Fishes: 2, 10, 13, 14, 17, 18, 19, 26, 28, 29, 31, 33, 34, 35 and 40 in the pictorial fish key, and all drawings in the pictorial invertebrate key are by Kim Odenweller.

The map on the inside of the front cover was drawn by Laurence L. Laurent.

All other drawings are by Daniel J. Miller.

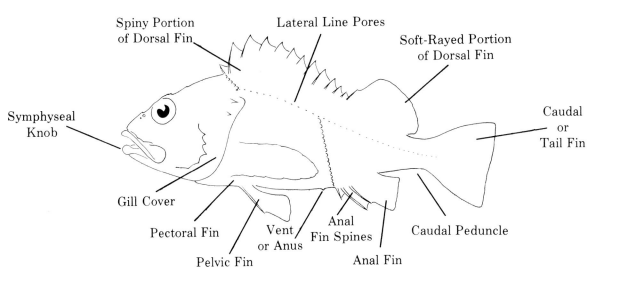

Spiny Portion of Dorsal Fin

Lateral Line Pores

Soft-Rayed Portion of Dorsal Fin

Caudal or Tail Fin

Symphyseal Knob

Gill Cover

Pectoral Fin

Pelvic Fin

Vent or Anus

Anal Fin Spines

Anal Fin

Caudal Peduncle

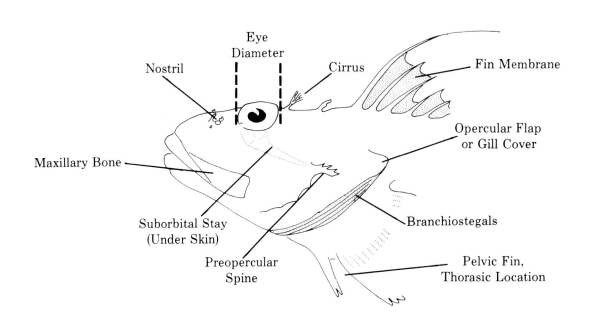

Eye Diameter

Nostril

Cirrus

Fin Membrane

Maxillary Bone

Opercular Flap or Gill Cover

Suborbital Stay (Under Skin)

Preopercular Spine

Branchiostegals

Pelvic Fin, Thorasic Location

Parts of a Bony Fish

(Drawings by Daniel J. Miller)

PICTORIAL KEY TO FISH FAMILIES

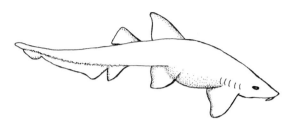

1. HAMMERHEAD SHARKS   P. 16

2. NURSE SHARKS   P. 16

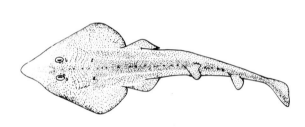

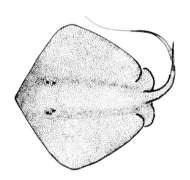

3. GUITARFISHES   P. 16

4. STINGRAYS   P. 16

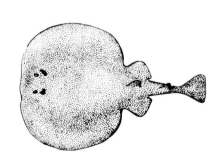

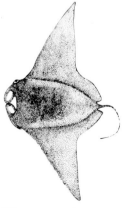

5. ELECTRIC RAYS   P. 18

6. MANTA RAYS   P. 18

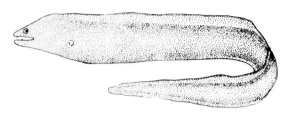

7. SNAKE EELS   P. 18   **8. MORAY EELS**   P. 20

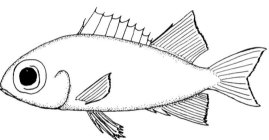

9. CONGER EELS   P. 22   **10. SQUIRRELFISHES**   P. 22

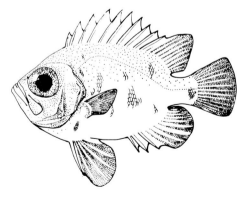

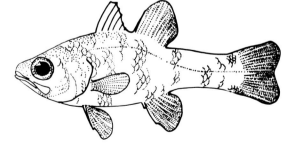

11. BIGEYES   P. 23   **12. CARDINALFISHES**   P. 24

13. CORNETFISH   P. 26

14. TRUMPETFISH   P. 26

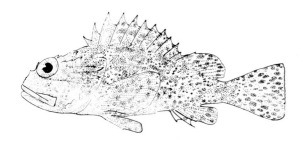

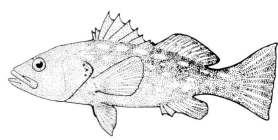

15. SCORPIONFISH   P. 26

16. SEA BASS   P. 26

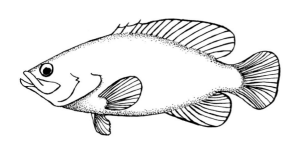

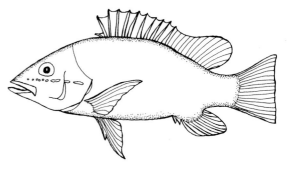

17. SOAPFISH   P. 32

18. SNAPPERS   P. 32

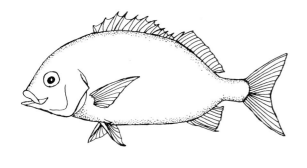

19. GRUNTS   P. 34

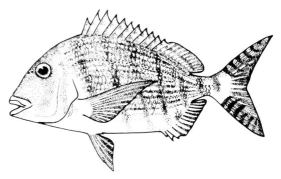

20. PORGYS   P. 36

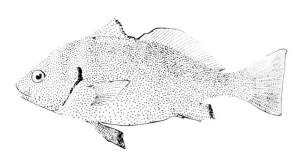

21. CROAKERS   P. 36

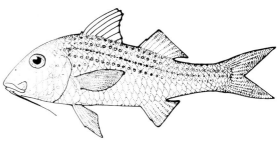

22. GOATFISH   P. 38

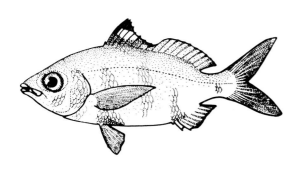

23. MOJARRAS   P. 38

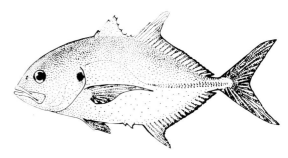

24. JACKS   P. 38

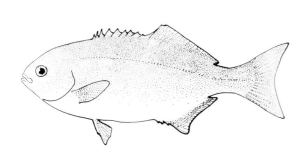

25. CHUBS P. 42

26. ANGELFISHES P. 44

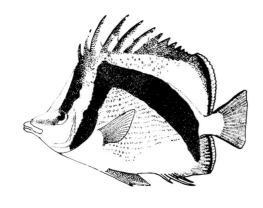

27. BUTTERFLYFISHES P. 48

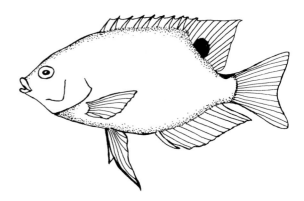

28. DAMSELFISHES P. 50

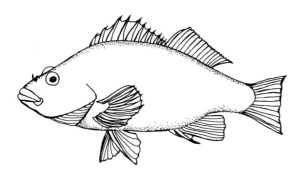

29. HAWKFISHES P. 55

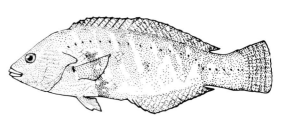

30. WRASSES P. 56

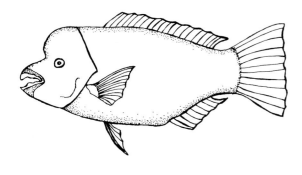

31. PARROTFISHES   P. 60

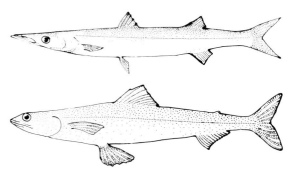

32. BARRACUDAS   P. 62

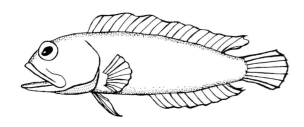

33. JAWFISH   P. 62

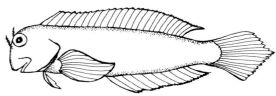

34. COMBTOOTH BLENNIES   P. 62

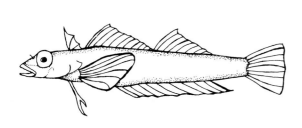

35. TRIPLEFIN BLENNIES   P. 64

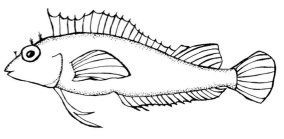

36. CLINID BLENNIES   P. 64

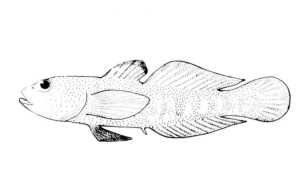

37. GOBIES P. 64

38. SURGEONFISHES P. 66

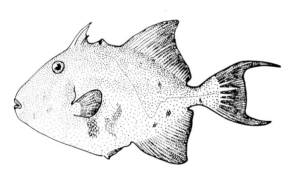

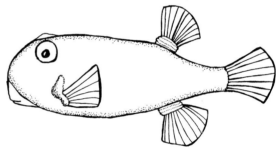

39. TRIGGERFISHES P. 68

40. TRUNKFISHES P. 72

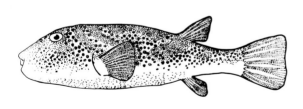

41. PUFFERS P. 72

42. PORCUPINEFISHES P. 74

FAMILY SPHYRNIDAE
Hammerhead Sharks
1. **SCALLOPED HAMMERHEAD (pez martillo)** *Sphyrna lewini*

(Hammer; after John Lewin, natural history painter)

Identification: The four lobes on the front margin of the head are the best field characters. *Size*: Length to 12 ft (3.7 m). *Habitat*: In surface waters around offshore reefs, sea mounts, and islands. *Range*: Southern California to Ecuador, including Hawaii.

FAMILY ORECTOLOBIDAE
Nurse Sharks
2. **NURSE SHARK** *Ginglymostoma cirratum*

(Hinged mouth, bearing cirri)

Identification: These bottom dwellers have a barbel near each nostril; lacks lower lobe on tail fin. *Size*: Length to 14 ft (4.3 m). *Habitat*: Soft bottoms around reefs; under ledges. *Range*: Tropical Atlantic and Pacific oceans. In Gulf of California at least from Isla Ceralvo and south.

FAMILY RHINOBATIDAE
Guitar Fishes
3. **BANDED GUITARFISH (pez guitarra)** *Zapteryx exasperata*

(Thin; made rough)

Identification: The disc, which is about as wide as long in adults, and many dark bands across the back separate this guitarfish from the shovelnose guitarfish, *Rhinobatus productus* (NI). *Size*: Length to 5.1 ft (1.6 m). *Habitat*: Soft bottoms around reefs; in caves in shallow water. *Range*: Newport Beach, California to Panama.

FAMILY DASYATIDAE
Stingrays
4. **DIAMOND STINGRAY (raya de espina)** *Dasyatis* sp.

(Rough or shaggy skate)

Identification: The diamond-shaped body and long tail with the sting closer to base than to the tip are good field characters. The two species, *D. brevis* (commonly called the longtailed diamond stingray) and *D. dipterura*, may be the same species. *Size*: Width to 5.8 ft (1.8 m). *Habitat*: Soft bottoms around reefs and in mangroves to depths of about 60 ft (18 m). *Range*: British Columbia to Peru, for both species.

5. **CORTEZ ROUND STINGRAY (raya manchada)** *Urolophus maculatus*

(Tail-crest; spotted)

Identification: Distinguished by a brownish disc covered with large black spots and light buff circular blotches. *Size*: Width to approximately 2 ft (0.6 m). *Habitat*: Shallow, sandy bottoms around islands and in bays. *Range*: Gulf of California.

1. SCALLOPED HAMMERHEAD

2. NURSE SHARK

3. BANDED GUITARFISH

4. DIAMOND STINGRAY

5. CORTEZ ROUND STINGRAY

6. **BULLSEYE STINGRAY (raya)** *Urolophus concentricus*

(Tail-crest: concentric)

Identification: Differs from Cortez Round Stingray in possessing dark markings that form concentric rings on outer edge of the disc; lacks black spots. *Size*: Width to about 2 ft (0.6 m). *Habitat*: Found on shallow, sandy areas around reefs and in bays. *Range*: Gulf of California.

FAMILY TORPEDINIDAE
Electric Rays

7. **TORPEDO RAY (raya electrica)** *Narcine entemedor*

(Numbness; intimidator)

Identification: Differs from Bullseye Electric Ray by possessing several large spots on back. *Size*: Length to 3 ft (0.9 m). *Habitat*: Shallow, soft bottoms around reefs and in bays. *Range*: Bahia Sebastian Viscaino, Baja California to Panama Bay.

8. **BULLSEYE ELECTRIC RAY (guitarra)** *Diplobatis ommata*

(Double-nostril fish; eyed)

Identification: Markings on the bullseye's back are very distinctive. *Size*: Length to about 1.5 ft (0.5 m). *Habitat*: Soft bottoms around reefs. *Range*: Gulf of California to Panama.

FAMILY MOBULIDAE
Manta Rays

9. **PACIFIC MANTA (manta raya)** *Manta hamiltoni*

(Blanket; after Captain Cospatrick Hamilton who first observed this ray)

Identification: The long lobes on either side of head, short tail (about equal to or shorter than body length) and generally large size, separate this pelagic plankton feeder from the smaller, long tailed (about twice body length) mobulas (NI). *Size*: Width to 25 ft (7.6 m). *Habitat*: Pelagic, often feeds around offshore reefs and rocks. *Range*: Santa Barbara Island, California to Peru.

FAMILY OPHICHTHIDAE
Snake Eels

10. **TIGER SNAKE EEL (anguilla)** *Myrichthys maculosus*

(Myrus-fish; spotted)

Identification: Presence of small pectoral fins, tubed nostrils, lack of rays in tip of tail, and one to three rows of large, black spots on body separate this eel from moray eels (Family Muraenidae) and other snake eels. *Size*: Length to 1.5 (0.5 m). *Habitat*: In and on shallow, sandy bottoms. *Range*: Throughout tropical Pacific, Indian Ocean and Red Sea.

11. **SPOTTED SNAKE EEL (morena)** *Ophichthus triserialis*

(Snake-fish; three rows)

Identification: A large mouth and variable sized dark spots on body separate this snake eel from the other snake eels in the Gulf. *Size*: Length to 3.7 ft (1.1 m). *Habitat*: Shallow, sandy bottoms. *Range*: Humboldt Bay, California to Peru.

6. BULLSEYE STINGRAY

7. TORPEDO RAY

8. BULLSEYE ELECTRIC RAY

9. PACIFIC MANTA

10. TIGER SNAKE EEL

11. SPOTTED SNAKE EEL

FAMILY MURAENIDAE
Morays

12. TIGER REEF EEL   *Uropterygius tigrinus*

(Tailfin; like a tiger in color)

Identification: Like all morays, this eel lacks pectoral and pelvic fins; the distinct, large, irregular spots distinguish it from other morays in the eastern Pacific. *Size*: Length to 4 ft (1.2 m). *Habitat*: Shallow reefs, usually in crevices. *Range*: Tropical Pacific; Islas Revillagigedos, and lower Gulf of California.

13. PANAMIC GREEN MORAY (morena verde)   *Gymnothorax castaneus*

(Naked breast; chestnut color)

Identification: Posterior nostrils lack tubes; dorsal fin well developed; greenish brown, occasionally with small, white spots. *Size*: Length to over 4 ft (1.2 m). *Habitat*: Crevices and holes during day; at night may be seen any place on reef or over sand or mud bottoms when foraging. *Range*: Gulf of California to Isla Malpelo, Columbia.

14. ZEBRA MORAY (morena cebra)   *Echidna zebra*

(Viper; zebra)

Identification: The members of this genus have blunt, molarlike teeth instead of sharp canine teeth. The only moray in the Gulf with white bands on a reddish brown body. *Size*: Length to 2.5 (0.8 m). *Habitat*: Crevices and holes, rocky reefs; occasionally found on sand bottoms. *Range*: Indo Pacific and from mid-Gulf to Panama.

15. JEWEL MORAY (morena pinta)   *Muraena lentiginosa*

(Moray; freckled)

Identification: Both the anterior and posterior nostrils are tubed in this genus; the chainlike rows of light spots ringed by dark brown halos are very distinctive on this nocturnal forager. *Size*: Length to 2 ft (0.6 m). *Habitat*: Crevices in reef during the day; anywhere on reef at night when foraging. *Range*: Central Gulf to Peru.

12. TIGER REEF EEL

13. ZEBRA MORAY

14. PANAMIC GREEN MORAY

15. JEWEL MORAY

FAMILY CONGRIDAE
Conger Eels

16. CORTEZ GARDEN EEL (anguila jardin) *Taeniconger digueti*

(Band, marine eel; after French naturalist Leon Diguet)

Identification: Differs from morays in having a small mouth, pectoral fins, and conspicuous lateral line pores. *Size*: Length to 2.1 ft (0.6 m). *Habitat*: Sand areas near reefs. *Range*: Central and lower Gulf of California.

FAMILY HOLOCENTRIDAE
Squirrelfishes

17. PANAMIC SOLDIERFISH (soldado) *Myripristis leiognathos*

(Myriad-saw; smooth jaw)

Identification: Distinguished by its bright red color and large eyes. *Size*: Length to 7 inches (17.8 cm). *Habitat*: During the day soldierfish can be found in caves and crevices; at night they forage around reefs. *Range*: Magdalena Bay and Gulf of California to Ecuador.

18. TINSEL SQUIRRELFISH (candil)   *Adioyryx suborbitalis*
(Without canal; below orbit of eye)

Identification: The prominent spine on the opercle separates this fish from the Panamic soldierfish; also the silvery body. *Size*: Length to 10 inches (25.4 cm). *Habitat*: Same as Panamic soldierfish. *Range*: Central Gulf of California to Ecuador.

FAMILY PRIACANTHIDAE
Bigeyes

19. GLASSEYE   *Priacanthus cruentatus*
(Saw-spine; bloody)

Identification: The large eye and reddish body with silver bars distinguish this nocturnal fish from other cave dwellers. *Size*: Length to 1.1 ft (0.3 m). *Habitat*: Caves and crevices. *Range*: Tropical western Atlantic and eastern Pacific, lower Gulf of California and Islas Revillagigedos.

FAMILY APOGONIDAE
Cardinalfishes

20. PINK CARDINALFISH — *Apogon parri*
(Without beard; after Professor A. E. Parr)

Identification: The dark bar below the second dorsal fin does not extend into dorsal fin of this nocturnal fish; lacks spot on caudal peduncle. *Size*: Length to about 2 inches (5 cm). *Habitat*: Caves and crevices during daylight, from shallow waters to about 100 ft (30 m). *Range*: The pink cardinalfish is the most common cardinalfish on the peninsula side of the Gulf of California from Loretto to Cabo San Lucas; it has been recorded as far south as Peru.

21. BARSPOT CARDINALFISH (cardenal) — *Apogon retrosella*
(Without beard; behind saddle)

Identification: Barspot cardinalfish possess both a bar, located below the second dorsal fin, and a tail spot. The bar extends upward into the dorsal fin. *Size*: Length to about 4 inches (10 cm). *Habitat*: This uncommon cardinalfish can be observed in the same habitat as the pink cardinalfish to depths of 200 ft (61 m). *Range*: Northern Gulf of California to Mazatlan and Cabo San Lucas. More common in the lower Gulf.

22. GUADALUPE CARDINALFISH — *Apogon guadalupensis*
(Without beard; Guadalupe Island)

Identification: Lacks both bar and spot. *Size*: Length to 5 inches (12.7 cm). *Habitat*: In caves and crevices to depths of 60 ft (18.3 m). *Range*: San Clemente Island, California to Cabo San Lucas.

23. PLAIN CARDINALFISH — *Apogon atricaudus*
(Without beard; black tail)

Identification: Similar to Guadalupe cardinalfish but possess a dark blotch on first dorsal fin. *Size*: Length to about 3 inches (7.6 cm). *Habitat*: By day, in crevices, caves, and among sea urchins; found to depths of about 100 ft (30 m). Feed in open at night. *Range*: Cabo San Lucas and Islas Revillagigedos.

A. Kirstich

20. PINK CARDINALFISH

21. EARSPOT CARDINALFISH

L. Laurent

22. GUADALUPE CARDINALFISH

23. PLAIN CARDINALFISH

FAMILY FISTULARIIDAE
Cornetfishes

24. REEF CORNETFISH (pex corneta)   *Fistularia commersonii*
(Tube; after P. Commerson, a French naturalist)

Identification: The shape of the body and the long filiment protruding from the caudal fin are very distinctive. A deeper water cornetfish also occurs in the Gulf of California, but it differs from the reef cornetfish by having more rays in the dorsal, anal, and pectoral fins, thus the two cannot be differentiated underwater. *Size*: Length to about 4 ft (1 m). *Habitat*: Around reefs and wrecks to depths of about 100 ft (30 m). *Range*: Western Indian Ocean to Eastern Tropical Pacific; from Gulf of California and Bahia Magdalena to Panama.

FAMILY AULOSTOMIDAE
Trumpetfishes

25. TRUMPETFISH   *Aulostomus chinensis*
(Tube mouth; China)

Identification: Similar to cornetfish, but this predator on small fish possesses a barbel on the chin, and lacks the long caudal fin filament. *Size*: Length to about 4 ft (1 m). *Habitat*: Occurs around coral and rocky reefs. *Range*: Tropical western and eastern Pacific, including Islas Revillagigedos, but not recorded from the Gulf of California.

FAMILY SCORPAENIDAE
Scorpionfishes

26. STONE SCORPIONFISH (lapon)   *Scorpaena mystes*
(Scorpion; priest)

Identification: The head is covered with numerous skin flaps or large cirri, which are lacking in the two other shallow water scorpionfishes that occur along the Baja Peninsula, the spotted scorpionfish, *Scorpaena guttata*, and rainbow scorpionfish, *Scorpaenodes xyris* (NI). *Size*: Length to 1.5 ft (0.5 m). *Habitat*: Shallow reefs and sandy areas. *Range*: Bahia Sebastian Vizcaino and Gulf of California to Ecuador.

FAMILY SERRANIDAE
Sea Basses

27. GULF GROUPER (baya)   *Mycteroperca jordani*
(Nostril-fish; after David Starr Jordan)

Identification: Adults are grayish; juveniles have blotches. Differs from the jewfish, *Epinephelus itajara* (NI) by having a square tail and larger eye. The profile of the anal fin is straight to convex; both tail and anal fins have white margins. *Size*: Length to 5 ft (1.5 m). *Habitat*: Rocky reefs and sand bottoms; in caves and crevices, in depths of 15 to over 100 ft (4.6 to 30 m). *Range*: Southern California and Gulf of California.

28. SAWTAIL GROUPER   *Mycteroperca prionura*
(Nostril-fish; sawtail)

Identification: Jagged tail fin and large and small red-brown spots are distinctive; can be separated from the less common broomtail grouper, *M. xenarcha* (NI) by the color pattern: the broomtail grouper is brown to grayish-green with irregular dark blotches. *Size*: Length to about 3 ft (0.9 m). *Habitat*: Rocky reefs and caves. *Range*: Isla Santa Ines to Bahia Banderas.

24. REEF CORNETFISH

25. TRUMPET FISH

26. STONE SCORPIONFISH

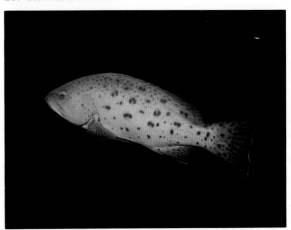

27. GULF GROUPER

28. SAWTAIL GROUPER

golden phase

29. LEOPARD GROUPER AND GOLDEN GROUPER (cabrilla sardinera and calamaria) *Mycteroperca rosacea*

(Nostril-fish; rosy)

Identification: Small reddish spots cover the body, forming a reticulated pattern; dorsal, anal, and pelvic fins have white margins. A few of the leopard groupers turn yellow gold (golden groupers), and these occasionally have small patches of dark pigment. *Size*: Length to 3 ft (0.9 m). *Habitat*: Rocky reefs to depths of about 150 ft (46 m). *Range*: Bahia Magdalena and Gulf of California to Puerta Vallarta.

30. SPOTTED CABRILLA (cabrilla pinta) *Epinephelus analogus*

(Clouded over; similar)

Identification: The rounded tail fin separates this fish from the leopard grouper. *Size*: Length to 2.5 ft (0.8 m). *Habitat*: Offshore reefs, in depths to 60 ft (18 m). *Range*: Southern California and Gulf of California to Peru.

31. FLAG CABRILLA (cabrilla piedrera)   *Epinephelus labriformis*
(Clouded over; form)

Identification: White spots on the olive-green to red-brown body and red margins on the soft dorsal, anal, and tail fins are very distinctive. *Size*: Length to 1.7 ft (0.5 m). *Habitat*: Rocky areas in depths to 100 ft (30 m). *Range*: Central Gulf of California to Peru.

32. PANAMA GRAYSBY (enjambre)   *Epinephelus panamensis*
(Clouded over; Panama)

Identification: Distinguished by the 9 to 10 dark bars on the body and blue and orange spots on the side of the head. *Size*: Length to at least 1 ft (0.3 m). *Habitat*: Rocky reefs and crevices to depths of 250 ft (76 m). *Range*: Gulf of California to Columbia.

33. MUTTON HAMLET (guaseta)

Epinephelus afer
(Clouded over; Africa)

Identification: The best field characters for this secretive and solitary fish are the marked color patterns of the red-brown body with light spots, the red eye, and the seven to eight transverse dark bars on the pectoral fins. *Size*: Length to 10 inches (25.4 cm). *Habitat*: Shallow reefs. *Range*: In the eastern Pacific from the upper Gulf of California to Peru; also occurs in western Atlantic.

34. LEATHER BASS — *Epinephelus dermatolepis*
(Clouded over; skin)

Identification: In adults, color pattern of white blotches and small dark spots on a gray background (occasionally with several dark bars) is very distinctive. Juveniles have dark bars on a white background. *Size*: Length to about 3 ft (0.9 m). *Habitat*: Around reefs to depths of at least 100 ft (30 m). *Range*: Abundant around Islas de Revillagigedos; uncommon to rare in Gulf (Isla San Pedro to Cabo San Lucas) south to Ecuador.

35. **BARRED SERRANO (serrano)** *Serranus fasciatus*

(Saw; banded)

Identification: The best field characters are the six pairs of dark bars, often condensed into a dark stripe above lateral line, and eight dark bars below lateral line. *Size*: Length to about 7 inches (17 cm). *Habitat*: Around reefs, on sandy bottoms, to depths of at least 200 ft (61 m). *Range*: Gulf of California to Peru and Islas Galapagos.

36. **PACIFIC CREOLEFISH (rabirrubia de lo alto)** *Paranthias colonus*

(Near-Anthias; colon, native name for similar fish)

Identification: Salmon-red color, deeply forked tail, and the four or five light spots on the back identify the adult. Juveniles are pinkish-yellow, the dorsal spots are bright blue. *Size*: Length to at least 14 inches (35.6 cm). *Habitat*: Around reefs, usually in schools; during daytime these foraging schools range throughout the water column. In depths to about 200 ft (61 m). *Range*: Commonly found from the central Gulf of California to Peru.

37. **PACIFIC SAND PERCH (cabaicucho)** *Diplectrum pacificum*

(Two-spur; Pacific)

Identification: The dark bars and two stripes on a yellow body and the black spot at the base of the tail are the best field characters. *Size*: Length to 9 inches (23 cm). *Habitat*: On sandy bottom around reefs to depths of at least 50 ft (15 m). *Range*: Bahia San Juanico and throughout the Gulf of California.

FAMILY GRAMMISTIDAE
Soapfish

38. **CORTEZ SOAPFISH (jabonero de Cortes)** *Rypticus bicolor*

(Washing; two-colored)

Identification: Best distinguished underwater by the rounded dorsal, anal, and caudal fins and brown body with light spots and blotches. *Size*: Lengths to about 1 ft (0.3 m). *Habitat*: In caves and crevices during the daytime; soapfish come out at night to feed on small fish around reefs and over sand bottoms. Depths to about 225 ft (6.9 m). *Range*: Gulf of California to Peru.

FAMILY LUTJANIDAE
Snappers

39. **YELLOW SNAPPER (pargo amarillo)** *Lutjanus argentiventris*

(Likeness; silver belly)

Identification: The yellow dorsal, anal, pectoral, and caudal fins, and the yellow rear half of the body are the best field identification characters for adults. The bright yellow juveniles are very distinctive. *Size*: Length to 2 ft (0.6 m). *Habitat*: Around reefs and over sand bottoms near reefs, also in caves; to depths of at least 75 ft (23 m). *Range*: Bahia Magdalena and from upper Gulf of California to Peru. One record from California.

35. BARRED SERRANO

36. PACIFIC CREOLFISH

37. PACIFIC SAND PERCH

38. CORTEZ SOAPFISH

juvenile   **39. YELLOW SNAPPER**   adult

40. **PACIFIC DOG SNAPPER (pargo prieto)** *Lutjanus novemfasciatus*
(Likeness; nine banded)

Identification: Can best be identified underwater by the large canine teeth, which are usually visible, and the nine obscure, dusky bars on a silvery body. Large adults are reddish when out of water. *Size*: Length to 3 ft (0.9 m). *Habitat*: In caves during the day; feed around reefs at night; to depths of at least 100 ft (30 m). *Range*: Gulf of California to Peru.

41. **BLUE-AND-GOLD SNAPPER (pargo rayado)** *Lutjanus viridis*
(Likeness; green)

Identification: The blue and gold stripes are very distinctive. *Size*: Length to 1 ft (0.3 m). *Habitat*: Schools occur around reefs to depths of about 50 ft (15 m). *Range*: This common snapper occurs from central Gulf (Isla Monserrate) to Ecuador.

42. **BARRED PARGO (coconaco)** *Hoplopagrus guntheri*
(Armor porgy; after Dr. Alfred Gunther)

Identification: The upper body is green-brown to dark brown; the lower body ranges from copper-red to maroon. There are eight or nine bars on the body. Juveniles have a dark spot below the rear of the soft dorsal fin. *Size*: Length to 2.5 ft (0.8 m). *Habitat*: Juveniles can be observed in mangrove swamps; adults occur around reefs, large boulders and caves. To depths of about 90 ft (27 m). *Range*: Occurs throughout Gulf of California and south to Panama.

FAMILY HAEMULIDAE
Grunts

43. **BURRITO GRUNT (burrito)** *Anisotremus interruptus*
(Unequal aperture; broken)

Identification: The sharp, slanting profile of the head, the fleshy lips, and large conspicuous scales with dark spots on their anterior margin readily identify this grunt. *Size*: Length to 1.5 ft (0.5 m). *Habitat*: The adults are found around reefs and in caves to depths of about 75 ft (23 m). *Range*: Bahia Magdalena and Gulf of California to Peru; common around Islas de Revillagigedos.

44. **GRAYBAR GRUNT (burro almejera)** *Haemulon sexfasciatum*
(Blood gum; six-banded)

Identification: The distinctive yellow and dark gray bars are the best field characters. *Size*: Length to 1.5 ft (0.5 m). *Habitat*: Around reefs, over sandy bottoms to depths of about 75 ft (23 m). *Range*: Gulf of California to Panama.

45. **CORTEZ GRUNT (burro de Cortes)** *Haemulon flaviguttatum*
(Blood-gums; yellow spotted)

Identification: The pearly-blue spot on each scale is the best character. *Size*: Length to 8.9 inches (22.6 cm). *Habitat*: Around reefs to depths of about 50 ft (15 m); and, commonly, in mangrove swamps. *Range*: Outer Baja coast (Bahia San Juanico) and Gulf of California to Panama.

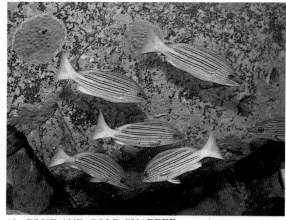

40. DOG SNAPPER

41. BLUE-AND-GOLD-SNAPPER

42. BARRED PARGO

43. BURRITO GRUNT

44. GRAYBAR GRUNT

45. CORTEZ GRUNT

46. SPOTTAIL GRUNT

Haemulon maculicauda
(Blood-gums; spot tail)

Identification: Distinguished by spots on scales that form stripes on sides, and the dusky blotch at the base of the tail fin. *Size*: Length to about 1 ft (0.3 m). *Habitat*: During the day, schools occur around reefs; at night these fish move off the reef to feed over sandy bottoms, in depths to at least 100 ft (30 m). *Range*: Gulf of California to Ecuador.

47. PANAMIC PORKFISH

Anisotremus taeniatus
(Unequal aperture; striped ribbon)

Identification: The distinctive color pattern of gold and blue stripes on the body readily identifies this fish. *Size*: Length to about 1 ft (0.3 m). *Habitat*: Around reefs to depths of at least 75 ft (23 m). *Range*: Cabo San Lucas area (Chileno Bay) to Ecuador.

FAMILY SPARIDAE
Porgies

48. PACIFIC PORGY (mojarron)

Calamus brachysomus
(Quill; short body)

Identification: Distinguished by the sharp, slanting profile of the head and deep body. *Size*: Length to 2 ft (0.6 m). *Habitat*: Usually found over sand around reefs to depths of 225 ft (69 m). *Range*: Oceanside, California and Gulf of California to Peru.

FAMILY SCIAENIDAE
Croakers

49. STRIPED CORVINA (corvina rayada)

Cynoscion reticulatus
(Dog-sciana; netted)

Identification: The many brown streaks or stripes on the silvery body are the best underwater characters. *Size*: Length to 2 ft (0.6 m). *Habitat*: A mid-water fish that occasionally feeds around shallow reefs and offshore rocks. *Range*: Gulf of California to Panama.

50. ROCK CROAKER (gungo)

Pareques viola
(Horseman; violet)

Identification: The light to dark brown coloration and high first dorsal fin identify the adults; the yellow-and-black striped juveniles are very distinctive. *Size*: Length to about 10 inches (25 cm). *Habitat*: In caves and crevices to depths of at least 100 ft (30 m). *Range*: Gulf of California to Panama, including Islas Revillagigedos.

46. SPOTTAIL GRUNT

47. PANAMIC PORKFISH

48. PACIFIC PORGY

49. STRIPED CORVINA

50. ROCK CROAKER   **adult**

37

FAMILY MULLIDAE
Goatfish

51. **MEXICAN GOATFISH (salmonete)**   *Mulloidichthys dentatus*

(A kind of fish; toothed)

Identification: The yellow stripe running from the eye to the tail readily identifies this goatfish. At night the body is covered with reddish blotches, but the yellow stripe is still visible. *Size*: Length to about 1 ft (0.3 m). *Habitat*: Usually over sandy bottoms around reefs to depths of at least 75 ft (23 m). *Range*: Southern California and the Gulf of California to Peru, including the offshore islands.

FAMILY GERREIDAE
Mojarras

52. **PACIFIC FLAGFIN MOJARRA (mojarra or charrita)**   *Eucinostomus* sp.

(To move mouth well)

Identification: Distinguished by the long snout with a protrusible mouth and the black-and-white markings on the first dorsal fin. *Size*: Length to 6 inches (15.2 cm). *Habitat*: Shallow, sandy bottoms in bays and mangrove swamps. *Range*: Southern California and Gulf of California south to Peru.

FAMILY CARANGIDAE
Jacks

53. **PACIFIC CREVALLE JACK (toro)**   *Caranx caninus*

(Head; canine-like)

Identification: The black spot on the rear of the gill cover, the white tip on both the soft dorsal and anal fins, and the deep body readily identify this pelagic, inshore jack. *Size*: Length to 2.5 ft (0.8 m) and weight to 50 lb (23 kg). *Habitat*: Commonly occurs around reefs. *Range*: Worldwide in tropical seas; on this coast from San Diego, California to Peru.

51. MEXICAN GOATFISH

52. FLAGFIN MOJARRA

53. PACIFIC CREVALLE JACK

54. BLUE-SPOTTED JACK

Caranx melamphygus
(Head; black rump)

Identification: The blue-and-black spots on a silvery body are very distinctive on this pelagic jack. *Size*: Length to at least 3 ft (0.9 m). *Habitat*: Found around reefs. *Range*: Tropical Indo-Pacific; in eastern Pacific from Cabo San Lucas and Islas Revillagigedos to Panama.

55. BROWN JACK (jurel negro)

Caranx lugubris
(Head; mournful)

Identification: The brown to black color is the best underwater character for this near-shore, pelagic jack. *Size*: Length to at least 3 ft (0.9 m). *Habitat*: Frequently found around reefs and islands. *Range*: World-wide in tropical waters; common around Islas Revillagigedos.

56. GOLD-SPOTTED JACK *Carangoides ferdau*

(Head-likeness; native common name in Red Sea area)
Identification: The gold spots above and below the lateral line, but located below the center of soft dorsal fin is the best underwater character. *Size*: Length to about 2 ft (0.6 m). *Habitat*: Found around reefs. *Range*: Tropical Indo-Pacific, Hawaii, and Islas Revillagigedos.

57. PACIFIC AMBERJACK (pez fuerte) *Seriola colburni*

(Italian name for a member of the genus; after A. E. Colburn)
Identification: This pelagic jack can be distinguished underwater from the yellowtail, *Seriola lalandi*, (NI) by the lack of a yellow tail and the dark bar that runs through the eye. *Size*: Length to about 5 ft (1.5 m). *Habitat*: Frequently found around reefs. *Range*: Oceanside, California to and in the Gulf of California to Peru, including Islas de Revillagigedos.

58. GREEN JACK (cocinero dorado)   *Caranx caballus*
(Head; horse)

Identification: Differs from other *Caranx*-type jacks by its longer, more slender body. *Size*: Length to 1.3 ft (0.4 m). *Habitat*: Commonly found around reefs. *Range*: Santa Cruz Island, California to and in Gulf of California to Peru.

59. GAFFTOPSAIL POMPANO (pompanito)   *Trachinotus rhodopus*
(Rough back; rose-colored foot)

Identification: The only jack having soft dorsal and anal fin rays that reach beyond the base of tail fin if laid flat. *Size*: Length to 2 ft (0.6 m). *Habitat*: Commonly found around reefs. *Range*: Zuma Beach, California to Gulf of California and Peru.

FAMILY KYPHOSIDAE
Sea Chubs

60. GULF OPALEYE (ojo azul)   *Girella simplicidens*
(A small wrasse; simple tooth)

Identification: The dark body, bright blue eyes, and the three to four white spots on the sides just below the dorsal fin are good field characters for this abundant upper Gulf of California fish. *Size*: Length to about 1.5 ft (0.5 m). *Habitat*: Shallow reefs in areas where algae is abundant. *Range*: Gulf of California.

61. BLUE-BRONZE CHUB   *Kyphosus analogus*
(A hump; resembles)

Identification: Can best be distinguished from the other chub that occurs in the Gulf of California by the presence of an orange stripe that runs from the upper jaw, under the eye, to the back edge of the gill cover. The thin, light orange stripes on the sides are also good field characters. *Size*: Length to 1.5 ft (0.5 m). *Habitat*: Around shallow reefs. *Range*: Oceanside, California to the Gulf of California and Peru.

62. CORTEZ CHUB (chopa de Cortes)   *Kyphosus elegans*
(Hump; elegant)

Identification: Lacks the orange stripe under eye and orange body stripes of the blue-bronze chub. Instead has a faint dark stripe under the eye. *Size*: Length to 1.3 ft (0.4 m). *Habitat*: Around shallow reefs. *Range*: Gulf of California to Panama.

63. SOCORRO CHUB   *Kyphosus lutescens*
(Hump; growing yellow)

Identification: Dark phase is indistinguishable from the Cortez Chub, but the golden color phase is unique; about 1 of 10 Socorro chubs are in golden phase. *Size*: Length to about 1.3 ft (0.4 m). *Habitat*: Shallow reefs to depths of about 100 ft (30 m). *Range*: Known from the Islas Revillagigedos.

58. GREEN JACK

59. GAFFTOPSAIL POMPANO

A. Kirstitch

60. GULF OPALEYE

61. BLUE-BRONZE CHUB

62. CORTEZ CHUB

63. SOCORRO CHUB

64. **ZEBRA PERCH (chopa bonita)** *Hermosilla azurea*

(Capitol of State of Sonora, Mexico; sky blue)

Identification: The scales on head and the presence of bars on the body separate this fish from all other members of the family. *Size*: Length to 1.4 ft (0.4 m). *Habitat*: Shallow reefs, particularly in the mid- and upper-Gulf. *Range*: Monterey, California to Gulf of California.

FAMILY POMACANTHIDAE
Angelfishes

65. **CORTEZ ANGELFISH (ángel de cortés)** *Pomacanthus zonipectus*

(Gill cover spine; zone breast)

Identification: The gray body of adults, with yellow-and-black bands on the head and anterior body, and the yellow-and-black bands on the head and body of juveniles are distinctive characters. *Size*: Length to 1.5 ft (0.5 m). *Habitat*: Around reefs to depths of at least 100 ft (30 m). *Range*: Upper Gulf of California to Peru.

64. ZEBRA PERCH

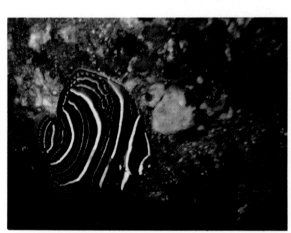

juvenile

65. CORTEZ ANGELFISH

adult

juvenile

adult

66. CLARION ANGELFISH *Holacanthus clarionensis*

(Whole spine; Clarion Island)

Identification: The bright orange body and tail of the adults are very distinctive. Juveniles resemble juvenile king angelfish, but differ in having an orange head and tail. *Size*: Length to 1 ft (0.3 m). *Habitat*: Rocky and coral reefs to depths of about 100 ft (30 m). *Range*: From Isla Espirito de Santos, in the Gulf of California, to Islas Revillagigedos.

juvenile

adult

67. KING ANGELFISH (ángel real) *Holacanthus passer*
(Whole spine; a sparrow)

Identification: The adults have a yellow tail and a vertical white bar on the sides just behind the origin of the pectoral fin. Juveniles have more yellow on the body and yellow pelvic fins. *Size*: Length to 1.2 ft (0.4 m). *Habitat*: Around shallow reefs to depths of about 160 ft (49 m). *Range*: Central Gulf of California and from Isla Guadalupe on outer coast to Ecuador.

47

FAMILY CHAETODONTIDAE
Butterflyfishes

68. THREEBANDED BUTTERFLYFISH (muñeca) *Chaetodon humeralis*
(Bristle tooth; shoulder)

Identification: The three dark bars on a silvery body are very distinctive. *Size*: Length to 10 inches (25.4 cm). *Habitat*: Usually around reefs and wrecks; to depths of about 180 ft (55 m). *Range*: Southern California (one record) and Bahia Kino in the Gulf of California south to Peru.

69. SCYTHE BUTTERFLYFISH *Chaetodon falcifer*
(Bristle tooth; scythe bearer)

Identification: The high, spinous dorsal fin, long snouth, and scythe-shaped black markings on sides of body are very distinctive. *Size*: Length to 6 inches (15.2 cm). *Habitat*: Deep reefs and kelp beds; in depths of 35 to 250 ft (11 to 76 m). *Range*: Santa Catalina Island, California to Islas Galapagos; common around San Benitos islands.

70. LONGNOSE BUTTERFLYFISH *Forcipiger flavissimus*
(Tweezer bearer; very yellow)

Identification: Easily recognized by the long, slender snout, yellow body, and black tail. *Size*: Length to 6 inches (15.2 cm). *Habitat*: Rocky reefs to depths of about 75 ft (23 m). *Range*: Gulf of California from La Paz to Cabo San Lucas, Islas Revillagigedos, and throughout Indo-Pacific region.

71. BARBERFISH (barbero) *Johnrandallia nigrirostris*
(After John Randall; black beak)

Identification: The black forehead and the silvery-yellow body with the stripe under the dorsal fin are the best field characters. *Size*: Length to 8 inches (20.3 cm). *Habitat*: Shallow rock and coral reefs; to depths of about 130 ft (40 m). *Range*: Central Gulf of California to Panama, including offshore islands.

68. THREEBANDED BUTTERFLYFISH

69. SCYTHE BUTTERFLYFISH

70. LONGNOSE BUTTERFLYFISH

71. BARBERFISH

FAMILY POMACENTRIDAE
Damselfishes

72. CORTEZ DAMSELFISH   *Eupomacentrus rectifraenum*
(Pez azul de Cortés)   (Genuine gill cover spine; straight bridle)

Identification: The best character for the adults is the brown body; fin margins occasionally retain the iridescent blue of the juveniles, which can be separated from other damselfish juveniles by the black spot at the base of the soft dorsal fin and the spot on the dorsal side of the caudal peduncle. *Size*: Length to about 5 inches (13 cm). *Habitat*: Shallow reefs in the central Gulf to depths of about 75 ft (23 m). *Range*: Gulf of California.

73. BEAUBRUMMEL (pez de dos colores)   *Eupomacentrus flavilatus*
(Genuine gill cover spine; yellow side)

Identification: The adults resemble Cortez damselfish but the fin margins are usually yellow. Juveniles are easily identified by the bright blue upper body and yellow lower body. *Size*: Length to 4 inches (10.2 cm). *Habitat*: Solitary juveniles and adults occur around reefs to depths of about 125 ft (38 m). *Range*: Central Gulf of California (Isla Danzante) to Ecuador.

74. CLARION DAMSELFISH   *Eupomacentrus redemptus*
(Genuine gill cover spine: redeem)

Identification: The juveniles resemble the whitetail damselfish, but the body is yellowish and the body scales have dark margins which give them a reticulated appearance. *Size*: Length to about 5 inches (13 cm). *Habitat*: Around shallow reefs. *Range*: Cabo San Lucas (rare) and Islas Revillagigedos.

72. CORTEZ DAMSELFISH   juvenile   adult

73. BREAUBRUMMEL   juvenile   adult

74. CLARION DAMSELFISH   adult

75. WHITETAIL DAMSELFISH — *Eupomacentrus leucorus*
(Genuine gill cover spine; white margin)

Identification: The adults have white to yellow margins on the pectoral fins and a pale band across the caudal peduncle. The juveniles are more iridescent and the greenish back coloration is more brilliant than on the adults. *Size*: Length to about 5 inches (13 cm). *Habitat*: This species is another reef dweller, found to depths of about 50 ft (15 m). *Range*: Cabo San Lucas and Isla San Jose to Islas Revillagigedos and Mazatlan; also recorded from Isla Guadalupe.

76. PANAMIC SERGEANT MAJOR (pintano) — *Abudefduf troschelii*
(Arabic name of a butterflyfish; after Professor Troschel)

Identification: The five or six black bars on a silver to yellow body are good field characters. *Size*: Length to 9 inches (22.9 cm). *Habitat*: Large aggregations occur around and over reefs and wrecks to depths of about 100 ft (30 m). *Range*: Gulf of California to Peru, including the offshore islands.

77. SCISSORTAIL DAMSELFISH (castaneta) — *Chromis atrilobata*
(Neigh fish; black lobed)

Identification: The best field characters are the deeply forked tail and the white spot below the soft dorsal fin. *Size*: Length to 5 inches (12.7 cm). *Habitat*: These damselfish congregate in large numbers around reefs; found to depths of about 250 ft (76 m). *Range*: Upper Gulf of California to northern Peru, including Islas Revillagigedos and Galapagos.

78. BLUE-AND-YELLOW CHROMIS — *Chromis limbaughi*
(Neigh fish; after Conrad Limbaugh)

Identification: The best field characters are the bright blue anterior body and the yellow dorsal fin and posterior upper body. *Size*: Length to about 6 inches (15 cm). *Habitat*: Aggregations occur around reefs to depths of about 225 ft (69 m). *Range*: Bahia de Los Angeles to Cabo San Lucas.

79. SILVERSTRIPE CHROMIS — *Chromis alta*
(Neigh fish; deep)

Identification: The iridescent blue juveniles resemble Cortez damselfish juveniles but lack the dark spot beneath the soft dorsal fin. Adults retain some of the blue markings but also have white lines at the base of the dorsal and anal fins. The dorsal surface of the caudal peduncle and the base of the caudal fin are white. *Size*: length to about 5 inches (13 cm). *Habitat*: Found around deeper reefs to depths of about 200 ft (61 m). *Range*: Islas San Benitos* to Cabo San Lucas; Isla Catalina in Gulf of Californa to Islas Galapagos.

75. WHITETAIL DAMSELFISH   **juvenile**   **adult**

76. PANAMIC SERGEANT MAJOR

77. SCISSORTAIL DAMSELFISH

78. BLUE-AND-YELLOW CHROMIS   **juvenile** **79. SILVERSTRIPE CHROMIS**   **juvenile**

juvenile

adult

80. GIANT DAMSELFISH   *Microspathodon dorsalis*
(castañuela gigante)   (Small sheath tooth; pertaining to back)

Identification: Adults are distinguished by the long dorsal, caudal, and anal fin rays; adult males have silvery-white heads. The juveniles are identified by iridescent blue spots on a dark body. *Size*: Length to 1 ft (0.3 m). *Habitat*: Gulf damselfish live around reefs; to depths of about 75 ft (23 m). *Range*: Central Gulf of California to Columbia.

81. BUMPHEAD DAMSELFISH   *Microspathodon bairdi*
(Small sheath tooth; after Spencer Fullerton Baird)

Identification: Distinguished by blue eyes, the bump on the head and the lack of filamentous dorsal, caudal, and anal fins. Juveniles resemble young beaubrummel, having bright, iridescent blue above and bright orange below. *Size*: Length to about 1 ft (0.3 m). *Habitat*: Found around reefs. *Range*: Central Gulf of California south to Ecuador; common around Cabo San Lucas.

FAMILY CIRRHITIDAE
Hawkfishes

82. GIANT HAWKFISH (chino mero)   *Cirrhitus rivulatus*
(Barbel; marked by rill-like streaks)
Identification: The brown bands on a gray-brown body and maze of wavy blue lines on the body and fins are good field characters. *Size*: Length to 1.7 ft (0.5 m). *Habitat*: Commonly observed on reefs, at the edge of crevices, and at entrance to caves; to depths of about 75 ft (23 m). *Range*: Upper Gulf of California to Columbia.

83. CORAL HAWKFISH   *Cirrhitichthys oxycephalus*
(halcon de coral)   (Barbel mouth fish; sharp head)
Identification: The red spots on a whitish background are good field characters. *Size*: Length to 3 inches (7.6 cm). *Habitat*: Occur on coral heads or around crevices and small rocks; to depths of about 75 ft (23 m). *Range*: Tropical Indo-Pacific, on this coast from the central Gulf of California (Isla Santa Ines) to Columbia, including the offshore islands.

84. **LONGNOSE HAWKFISH**   *Oxycirrhites typus*
                                                      (Sharp barbel; type)
Identification: The coloration of this hawkfish is similar to the coral hawkfish, but the long pointed snout distinguishes it from that species. *Size*: Length to about 3 inches (8 cm). *Habitat*: This deep-water hawkfish seems to prefer the gorgonians with yellow polyps that occur in depths of about 90 to 100 ft (27 to 30 m). *Range*: Tropical Pacific Ocean.

FAMILY LABRIDAE
Wrasses

85. **CHAMELEON WRASSE (señorita camaleón)**   *Halichoeres dispilus*
                                              (Pig-of-the-sea; two-spot)
Identification: The pink body, salmon-colored head and caudal fin, and green or blue spot just above the center of the pectoral fin are very distinctive. *Size*: Length to 8 inches (20. 3 cm). *Habitat*: Prefer shallow reef areas adjacent to sandy bottoms; found to depths of about 250 ft (76 m). *Range*: Gulf of California to Peru.

86. **SPINSTER WRASSE (soltera)**   *Halichoeres nicholsi*
                              (Pig-of-the-sea; after Captain Henry E. Nichols, U.S.N)
Identification: The male is darker on the anterior of a bluish-green body and has a yellow blotch anterior to the bar (fish from the Islas Revillagigedos have the yellow blotch on the gill cover); the female has a black bar that meets a black body stripe. Juveniles have a pale-yellow body with dark blotches. *Size*: Length to 1.3 ft (0.4 m). *Habitat*: Adults prefer reefs associated with sandy bottoms; found to depths of about 175 ft (53 m). *Range*: Gulf of California to Panama, including the offshore islands.

87. **WOUNDED WRASSE (señorita herida)**   *Halichoeres chierchiae*
                                        (Pig-of-the-sea; Italian woman's name)
Identification: Adults males are best identified by the dark-green spot with a red blotch behind the pectoral fin. The females have yellowish bands on the body and an orange tail. *Size*: Length to 8 inches (20.3 cm). *Habitat*: These fish prefer shallow reefs that support growths of algae and that are surrounded by sand patches; occasionally found to depths of 225 ft (69 m). *Range*: Puerta Penasco in upper Gulf to Acapulco.

G. Aeschliman

84. LONGNOSE HAWKFISH

85. CHAMELEON WRASSE

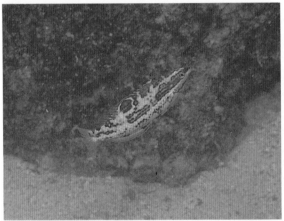

86. SPINISTER WRASSE　　　　　**juvenile**

female

male

87. WOUNDED WRASSE　　　　　**male**

57

88. CORTEZ RAINBOW WRASSE (arco iris)   *Thalassoma lucasanum*

(Sea green; refers to Cabo San Lucas)

Identification: The distinctive yellow and red stripes are the best field characters. Secondary males have purple heads and a yellow band just behind the head. *Size*: Length to 6 inches (15.2 cm). *Habitat*: Shallow reefs to depths of about 160 ft* (40 m). *Range*: Central Gulf of California to Islas Malpelo, Columbia.

89. SUNSET WRASSE   *Thalassoma lutescens*

(Sea green; growing yellow)

Identification: Identified by the green head, with wavy pink lines radiating from the eye, and the greenish-blue body. *Size*: Length to 8 inches (20.3 cm). *Habitat*: Found around shallow reefs to depths of about 75 ft (23 m). *Range*: Central Gulf of California to Panama; the most common wrasse to be found around the shallow reefs of Islas Revillagigedos.

90. PACIFIC RAZORFISH (viejita)   *Hemipteronotus pavoninus*

(Half fin back; like a peacock)

Identification: The two very long spines of the first dorsal fin and distinctive body shape distinguish this wrasse from the others in the Gulf of California. *Size*: Length to 10 inches (25.4 cm). *Habitat*: Both adults and juveniles occur over and in shallow sandy bottoms. These fish can actually swim within the sand. *Range*: Indo-west Pacific, Cabo San Lucas to Panama.

88. CORTEZ RAINBOW WRASSE females

juvenile secondary male

89. SUNSET WRASSE

90. PACIFIC RAZORFISH adult

91. MEXICAN HOGFISH (vieja)   *Bodianus diplotaenia*

(Portuguese name for labroid fishes; double band)

Identification: This fish can best be identified by the large fleshy hump on the head of the males and the two dark stripes on the bright yellow body of both juveniles and females. *Size*: Length to 2.5 ft (0.8 m). *Habitat*: These large wrasses prefer shallow reefs, but they have been recorded to depths of about 250 ft (76 m). *Range*: Isla Guadalupe and Gulf of California to Chile.

FAMILY SCARIDAE
Parrotfishes

92. BUMPHEAD PARROTFISH (perico)   *Scarus perrico*

(To pasture; parrot)

Identification: The best field characters for adults are the large hump on the head and the rounded posterior edge of the tail fin. *Size*: Length to 2.5 ft (76.2 cm). *Habitat*: Occurs on rocky reefs to depths of about 100 ft (30 m). *Range*: Central Gulf (Isla Carmen) to Peru.

93. BICOLOR PARROTFISH (perico)   *Scarus rubroviolaceus*

(To pasture; red violet)

Identification: Both adults are bicolored: males are dark green anteriorly and light green posteriorly; females are brownish-red anteriorly and light maroon to tan posteriorly. The posterior profile of the caudal fin is square, but the dorsal and ventral rays of the caudal fin extend beyond the rear edge. *Size*: length to 1.7 ft (0.5 m). *Habitat*: This parrotfish prefers reefs with abundant coral beds; found to depths of about 100 ft (30 m). *Range*: Tropical Indo-Pacific; on this coast, central Gulf of California (Isla Monserrate*) to Panama.

94. AZURE PARROTFISH (perico)   *Scarus compressus*

(To pasture; compressed)

Identification: Males have bright green bodies; each scale is outlined with orange; green streaks radiate from the eye. Juveniles of both sexes are reddish-brown. Adult females are light blue to blue-gray. The posterior edge of the tail fin is straight. *Size*: Length to 2 ft (0.6 m). *Habitat*: Occur around shallow reefs to depths of about 75 ft (23 m). *Range*: Bahia Concepción; central Gulf of California to Islas Galapagos.

91. MEXICAN HOGFISH   female   male

92. BUMPHEAD PARROTFISH   **93. BICOLOR PARROTFISH**

94. AZURE PARROTFISH   female   male

95. **BLUECHIN PARROTFISH (perico)** *Scarus ghobban*
(Arabian common name for this fish)
Identification: Females have light blue bands on a light orange-brown body. Males are bluish-green with a blue chin. The caudal fin is straight with longer upper and lower fin rays. *Size*: Length to 1.5 ft (0.5 m). *Range*: Indo-Pacific; on this coast from central Gulf of California (Isla Carmen) to Panama.

FAMILY SYNODONTIDAE
Lizardfishes

96. **LIZARDFISH** *Synodus* sp.
(Teeth meeting fish)
Identification: Lizardfishes can be identified by their long, lizardlike bodies and their habit of resting on their pelvic fins. *Size*: Length to about 1 ft (0.3 m). *Habitat*: Usually found on sandy bottoms in depths exceeding 60 ft (18 m). *Range*: Tropical seas.

FAMILY SPHYRAENIDAE
Barracudas

97. **MEXICAN BARRACUDA (picuda)** *Sphyraena ensis*
(Hammer fish; sword)
Identification: The best field characters are the long, slender body and large mouth with many teeth. *Size*: Length to about 2 ft (0.6 m). *Habitat*: Occur in large schools in surface waters around reefs, wrecks, and other structures. *Range*: Gulf of California to Panama.

FAMILY OPISTOGNATHIDAE
Jawfishes

98. **FINESPOTTED JAWFISH** *Opistognathus punctatus*
(boca grand manchada) (Behind jaw; spotted)
Identification: This, the largest of the Gulf of California jawfishes, can be identified by the fine dark spots on the head and large dark spots on body. *Size*: Length to 1.3 ft (0.4 m). *Habitat*: Jawfish construct burrows in shallow, sandy bottoms. *Range*: Bahia Magdalena and the Gulf of California to Panama.

FAMILY BLENNIIDAE
Combtooth Blennies

99. **PANAMIC FANGED BLENNY** *Ophioblennius steindachneri*
(trambollito negro) (Snake blenny; after Franz Steindachner)
Identification: The red ring around the eye, the dark spot behind the eye, and the blunt head are distinctive. *Size*: Length to 7 inches (17.8 cm). *Habitat*: Occur on reefs in shallow waters to depths of about 35 ft (11 m). *Range*: Bahia Sebastian Vizcaino and upper Gulf of California to Peru.

95. BLUECHIN PARROTFISH female

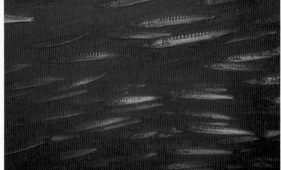

male

G. Aeschliman

96. LIZARDFISH

97. MEXICAN BARRACUDA

98. FINE SPOTTED JAWFISH

99. PANAMIC FANGED BLENNY

100. SABERTOOTH BLENNY (diente sable) *Plagiotremus azaleus*
(Oblique hole; parched)

Identification: The elongate yellow body, with two dark stripes, and a mouth located below and posterior to the snout are good field characters. *Size*: Length to 4 inches (10.2 cm). *Habitat*: Occur singly and in pairs with aggregations of rainbow wrasse, which their color pattern mimics, around reefs; to depths of about 50 ft (15 m). *Range*: Gulf of California to Peru, including offshore islands.

FAMILY TRIPTERYGIIDAE
Triplefin Blennies

101. LIZARD TRIPLEFIN *Genus and species undescribed*
(largartija tres aletas)

Identification: This most common of the Gulf triplefins can be distinguished by the three dorsal fins; the black mark on the caudal peduncle is preceeded by a white bar. *Size*: Length to about 4 inches (10 cm). *Habitat*: On reefs near crevices and under ledges; to depths of about 125 ft (38 m). *Range*: Gulf of California.

FAMILY CLINIDAE
Clinid Blennies

102. REDSIDE BLENNY (trambollo rojo) *Malacoctenus hubbsi*
(Soft comb; after Carl L. Hubbs, ichthyologist)

Identification: The pointed snout, the reddish marks on sides of the male, and the brownish broken stripes on the sides of juveniles and females are distinctive. *Size*: Length to 3.5 inches (8.9 cm). *Habitat*: On shallow reefs to depths of 25 ft (8 m). *Range*: Bahia Sebastian Vizcaino and Gulf of California to Acapulco.

103. LARGEMOUTH BLENNY (chalapo) *Labrisomus xanti*
(Labrus body; after John Xantus)

Identification: The large head and mouth, and the bright red throat of males during breeding season, are good field characters. *Size*: Length to 7 inches (17.8 cm). *Habitat*: In and around crevices on shallow reefs. *Range*: Bahia Sebastian Vizcaino and Gulf of California to Bahia Tenacatita Jalisco, Mexico.

104. ORANGETHROAT PIKEBLENNY *Chaenopsis alepidota*
(trambollito lucio) (To yawn face; scaleless)

Identification: The best field characters are the elongate body and the large mouth, i.e., the gape extends behind eye. *Size*: Length to 6 inches (15.2 cm). *Habitat*: Found in parchment worms' tubes in sandy, shelly bottoms near reefs; to depths of about 75 ft (23 m). *Range*: Gulf of California.

FAMILY GOBIIDAE
Gobies

105. BLUEBANDED GOBY (gobio bonito) *Lythrypnus dalli*
(Red sleeper; after W. H. Dall)

Identification: The color pattern of blue bands on the red body is very distinctive. *Size*: Length to 2.2 inches (5.6 cm). *Habitat*: This goby occurs around and in crevices, under ledges, and among sea urchin spines; found to depths of about 250 ft (76 m). *Range*: Morro Bay, California to and in Gulf of California.

100. SABERTOOTH BLENNY

101. LIZARD TRIPLEFIN

102. REDSIDE BLENNY

103. LARGE MOUTH BLENNY

104. ORANGETHROAT PIKE BLENNY

105. BLUEBANDED GOBY

106. REDHEAD GOBY (gobio de Cabeza rojo) *Elacatinus puncticulatus*
(Like a spindle; with fine specks)
Identification: The orange-red head of this goby has two black stripes, with a yellow stripe in between, extending posteriorly from the eye to at least the second dorsal fin *Size*: Length to 1.8 inches (4.6 cm). *Habitat*: Occurs on reefs, in crevices, and among sea urchin spines; found to depths of about 25 ft (8 m). Occasionally these gobies feed on parasites attached to other fish. *Range*: Upper Gulf of California to Ecuador.

107. BANDED CLEANER GOBY (gobio barbero) *Elacatinus diqueti*
(Like a spindle; after French naturalist Leon Diguet)
Identification: The distinctive orange-red head and the black bands on the body are the best field characters. *Size*: Length to 1.3 inches (3.3 cm). *Habitat*: In rocky crevices, where it cleans parasites from large fish such as moray eels and groupers; to depths of about 50 ft (15 m). *Range*: Isla Angel de la Guarda in the upper Gulf of California south to Columbia.

108. REDLIGHT GOBY (gobio semáforo) *Coryphopterus urospilus*
(Head fin; tail spot)
Identification: The dark spot at the base of the tail and the reddish spots on the whitish body identify this goby. *Size*: Length to 2.5 inches (6.4 cm). *Habitat*: Usually found on sand, around base of reefs to depths of about 125 ft (38 m). *Range*: Bahia Magdalena and the Gulf of California south to Columbia.

FAMILY ACANTHURIDAE
Surgeonfishes

109. CONVICT TANG *Acanthurus triostegus*
(Spine on tail; three to cover)
Identification: Six dark bars on a creamy-yellowish or white body are very distinctive. *Size*: Length to about 9 inches (23 cm). *Habitat*: Around shallow reefs, both alone and in small aggregations. *Range*: Tropical Indo-Pacific; on this coast from Bahia Los Frailes in the Gulf of California to Panama. They are very common around the Islas de Revillagigedos.

110. GOLDRIMMED SURGEONFISH *Acanthurus glaucopareius*
(Spine on tail; gray cheek)
Identification: The best field character is the bright yellow stripes along the base of the dorsal and anal fins. *Size*: Length to about 8 inches (20 cm). *Habitat*: Individuals occur around shallow reefs. *Range*: Tropical Pacific; on this coast from Cabo Pulmo* in the Gulf of California to Cabo San Lucas and Islas Revillagigedos.

106. REDHEAD GOBY

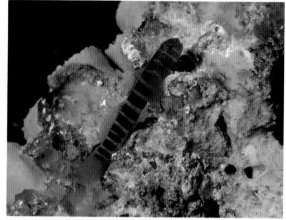

107. BANDED CLEANER GOBY

108. REDLIGHT GOBY

109.CONVICT TANG

110. GOLDRIMMED SURGEON FISH

111. YELLOWTAIL SURGEONFISH (cochinito)   *Prionurus punctatus*
(Saw-back; spotted)

Identification: The yellow tail and gray body, covered with black spots, is easily seen underwater. This surgeonfish can be distinguished from the very similar *P. laticlavius* (NI), the common yellowtail surgeonfish found around Clarion Islands which lack black spots. *Size*: Length to about 2 ft (0.6 m). *Habitat*: In groups around shallow reefs; to depths about 100 ft (30 m). *Range*: Upper Gulf of California to El Salvador, including offshore islands.

112. MOORISH IDOL (idolo moro)   *Zanclus canescens*
(A sickle; grayish)

Identification: The long snout, long filament on the dorsal fin, black vertical bands on body, and caudal fin are very distinctive. *Size*: Length to about 9 inches (23 cm). *Habitat*: These beautiful fish are usually found in pairs, around shallow reefs. *Range*: Tropical Indo-West Pacific; on this coast from La Paz to Panama.

FAMILY BALISTIDAE
Triggerfishes and Filefishes

113. REDTAIL TRIGGERFISH   *Xanthichthys mento*
(Cocklebur fish; having a long chin)

Identification: The red tail with a bright blue border and the streaks on the head are easily seen underwater. *Size*: Length to 10 inches (25.4 cm). *Habitat*: In mid water and near surface around reefs, anchored boats, and other structures; typically occur in large aggregations. *Range*: Tropical eastern Pacific, including Hawaiian Islands, and from Ventura, California to Clipperton Island. Very common around Islas Revillagigedos, but not recorded from the Gulf of California.

111. YELLOWTAIL SURGEON FISH

112. MOORISH IDOL

113. REDTAIL TRIGGER FISH

114. FINESCALE TRIGGERFISH (cochi)   *Balistes polyepis*
(To shoot; many scale)

Identification: The deep body, along with its drab coloration, distinguish this triggerfish. *Size*: Length to 2.5 ft (0.8 m). *Habitat*: Occurs in aggregations and singly around reefs as well as over sandy bottoms to depths of about 100 ft (30 m). Occasionally found at night lying on their sides. *Range*: Pt. Saint George, Del Norte County, California and Gulf of California south to Chile.

115. BLUNTHEAD TRIGGERFISH   *Pseudobalistes naufragium*
(False, balister; shipwreck)

Identification: Most easily identified by the dark bars on a bluish-gray to brownish-gray body and by the promiment forehead. *Size*: Length to at least 3 ft (0.9 m). *Habitat*: Occur around reefs and over sandy bottoms; to depths of about 100 ft (30 m). *Range*: Bahia San Quintin and in the Gulf of California from Isla San Francisco to Ecuador.

116. ORANGESIDE TRIGGERFISH (cochino)   *Sufflamen verres*
(An impediment; boar)

Identification: The brown body with the orange side patch and the shape of the body are distinctive field characters. *Size*: Length to about 1.3 ft (0.4 m). *Habitat*: Solitary fish occur around reefs and over sand patches. Found to depths of about 100 ft (30 m). *Range*: Cedros Island and in the Gulf from Isla Carmen to Ecuador.

117. BLACK DURGON   *Melichthys niger*
(Black fish; black)

Identification: A blue-black body with white stripes at the base of the dorsal and anal fins are the best field characters. *Size*: Length to about 1 ft (0.3 m). *Habitat*: This uncommon triggerfish occurs around shallow reefs. *Range*: Indo-Pacific, Isla San Francisco*; in the Gulf to Islas Revillagigedos, Clipperton, Cocos, and Malpelo Islands.

118. VAGABOND FILEFISH   *Cantherhines dumerili*
(Spine-snouth; after A.H.A. Domerell, French naturalist)

Identification: This fish is often confused with the surgeonfishes because of the sharp forward curving spines on the caudal peduncle. The spines are the best field character. *Size*: Length to about 1 ft (0.3 m). *Habitat*: Frequents shallow reefs. *Range*: Indo-Pacific; on this coast from Los Frailes in the Gulf to Islas Revillagigedos.

119. SCRAWLED FILEFISH   *Alutera scriptus*
(Sordid private deliver; written)

Identification: The bright blue-green scrawl marks and spots on the bluish-gray to olive-brown body and the shape of the body identify this fish. *Size*: Length to about 2 ft (0.6 m). *Habitat*: Around shallow reefs. *Range*: Worldwide tropical seas; on this coast it has been recorded from the central Gulf of California and Isla Revillagigedos.

114. FINESCALE TRIGGERFISH

115. BLUNTHEAD TRIGGERFISH

116. ORANGESIDE TRIGGERFISH

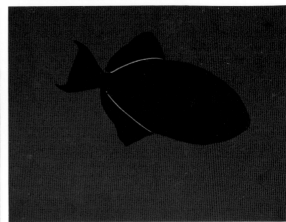

117. BLACK DURGON

118. VAGABOND FILEFISH

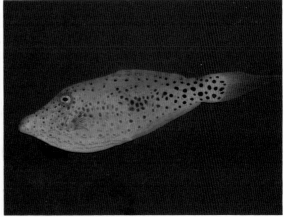

119. SCRAWLED FILEFISH

FAMILY OSTRACIIDAE
Boxfishes

120. PACIFIC BOXFISH (pex caja)

Ostracion meleagris
(Hard skin; guinea fowl)

Identification: The shape of the body, the placement of the dorsal and anal fins, and the different coloration of the male and female are distinctive. *Size*: Length to 7 inches (17. 8 cm). *Habitat*: Around shallow reefs. *Range*: Tropical Indo-Pacific; on this coast from Cabo Pulmo in the Gulf of California to Panama.

FAMILY TETRAODONTIDAE
Puffers

121. GUINEAFOWL PUFFER
(botete negro, and botete de oro)

Arothron Meleagris
(Plow; guinea fowl)

Identification: The black body with white spots and the occasional golden color phase are good field characters. *Size*: Length to about 1 ft (0.3 m). *Habitat*: Occurs around shallow reefs. *Range*: Tropical Pacific; on this coast from Isla San Diego in the Gulf of California to Ecuador.

female   120. PACIFIC BOXFISH   male

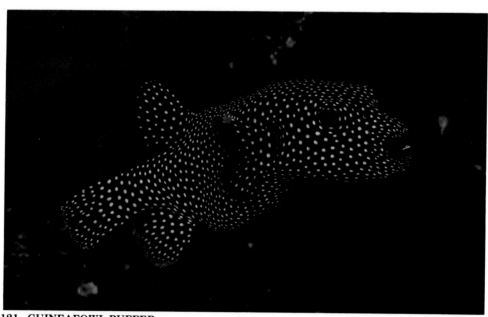

121. GUINEAFOWL PUFFER

122. SPOTTED SHARPNOSE PUFFER *Canthigaster punctatissima*
(botete bonito) (Spine belly; very much dotted)
Identification: The large, pointed snout and bluish-white spots on a reddish-brown body are distinguishing field characters. *Size*: Length to 3.5 inches (8.9cm). *Habitat*: Solitary individuals are found near crevices, caves and under ledges in shallow waters. *Range*: From Isla Carmen in the Gulf of California south to Panama, including the offshore islands.

123. BULLSEYE PUFFER (botete diana) *Sphoeroides annulatus*
(Sphere resemblence; ringed)
Identification: The best characters are distinctive body shape and concentric dark rings on the back. Both the sides and back are also covered with small dark spots. *Size*: Length to about 1.3 ft (0.4 m). *Habitat*: Shallow, sandy bottoms near reefs and in bays. *Range*: San Diego, California and the Gulf of California to Peru.

FAMILY DIODONTIDAE
Porcupinefishes

124. BALLOONFISH (pez erizo) *Diodon holocanthus*
(Two tooth: wholly spined)
Identification: The ballonfish is most easily recognized by the dark bar over the forehead that extends down past the eye and the long spines that cover the body and head. *Size*: Length to about 1.5 ft (0.5 m). *Habitat*: Shallow, sandy bottoms and around reefs. *Range*: Tropical seas, worldwide; very common in central and lower Gulf of California.

125. SPOTTED PORCUPINEFISH *Diodon hystrix*
(Two tooth; the porcupine)
Identification: This fish differs from the balloonfish by the lack of spines and the presence of a dark bar on the head. The body has more spotting. *Size*: Length to 3 ft (0.9 m). *Habitat*: This nocturnal porcupinefish is more secretive than the balloonfish, staying in caves and crevices during the day, and coming out at night to forage on the reef. *Range*: Warm seas of the world; on this coast from San Diego and in the Gulf of California to Chile.

122. SPOTTED SHARPNOSE PUFFER

123. BULLSEYE PUFFER

124. BALLOONFISH

125. SPOTTED PORCUPINEFISH

PICTORIAL KEY TO THE INVERTEBRATES

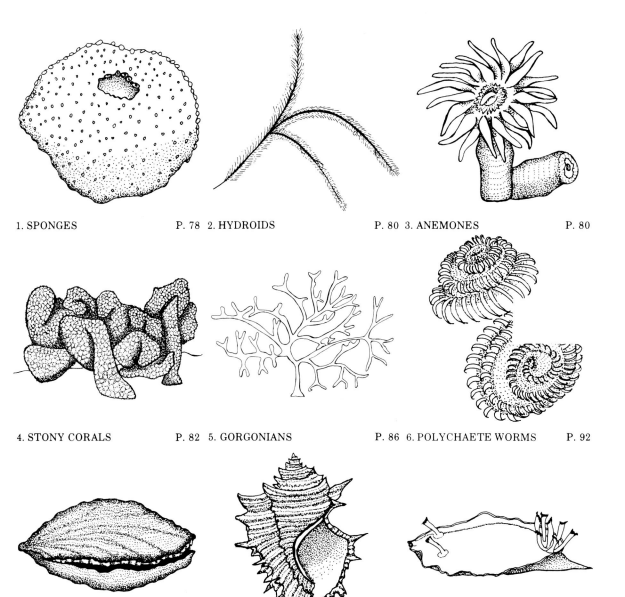

1. SPONGES   P. 78   2. HYDROIDS   P. 80   3. ANEMONES   P. 80

4. STONY CORALS   P. 82   5. GORGONIANS   P. 86   6. POLYCHAETE WORMS   P. 92

7. CLAMS   P. 92   8. SNAILS   P. 92   9. NUDIBRANCHS.   P. 94

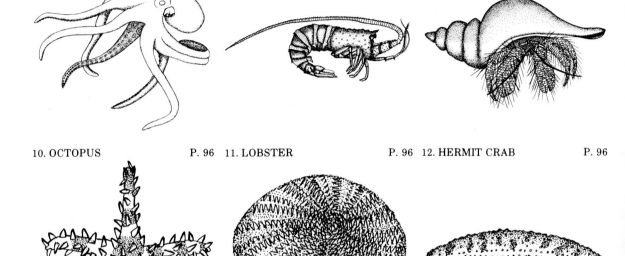

10. OCTOPUS   P. 96   11. LOBSTER   P. 96   12. HERMIT CRAB   P. 96

13. SEA STARS   P. 98   14. SEA URCHINS   P. 104   15. SEA CUCUMBER   P. 108

PHYLUM PORIFERA
Sponges

1. BARREL SPONGE

Pseudosuberites pseudos
(False cork-oak; false)

Identification: This large sponge is distinguished by an outer surface covered with large tubercles interspersed with craters and pits. There are only a few large excurrent pores (oscula). *Size*: Height to about 1 ft (30 cm) and diameter to about 1 ft (30 cm). *Habitat*: These colorful sponges occur on very shallow sandy and rocky bottoms. *Range*: Upper Gulf of California; common in Bahia de Los Angeles.

2. SULPHUR SPONGE

Verongia aurea
(True sponge; golden)

Identification: This common sponge varies greatly in form: three growth forms are illustrated. Color varies from yellow to orange to yellow-orange and brown. *Size*: Height to about 6 inches (15 cm). *Habitat*: Occur on rocks to depths of about 82 ft (25 m). Common in shallow waters of lower Gulf. *Range*: Cosmopolitan; occurs throughout Gulf of California and from Pt. Conception, California, to Cabo San Lucas.

1. BARREL SPONGE

a

b

2. SULPHUR SPONGE

c

PHYLUM CNIDARIA
Hydroids, Anemones, Corals, Gorgonians

3. **STINGING HYDROID**   ***Lytocarpus* sp.**

(Loosening fruit)

Identification: The best field character is the white, feather-like form of this hydroid, which may be the same species that occurs off Santa Catalina Island, California (*L. nuttingi*). This common subtidal hydroid is capable of inflicting painful stings; divers should avoid touching it with their bare skin. *Size*: Colonies may reach 1 ft in height (30 cm). *Habitat*: Shallow reefs to depths of about 60 ft (18 m). *Range*: Central and lower Gulf of California.

4. **BURROWING ANEMONE**   ***Pachycerianthus* spp.**

(Thick wax anemone)

Identification: The members of this genus are characterized by the parchment-like tube surrounding the column and the long tentacles. *Size*: Height to about 6 inches (15 cm). *Habitat*: Sand around reefs to depths of about 75 ft (23 m). *Range*: Gulf of California.

5. **SAND ANEMONE**   *Alicia beebei*

(From a woman's name; after W. H. Beebe, undersea explorer)

Identification: The long column and tentacles are the best field characters for this species when foraging at night (a). During daylight these anemones form groups with tentacles withdrawn (b). *Size*: Height to about 5 inches (13 cm). *Habitat*: Shallow sandy bottoms. *Range*: Central and lower Gulf of California.

3. STINGING HYDROID

4. BURROWING ANEMONE

5. SAND ANEMONE

6.   **ZOANTHID ANEMONE**   *Zoanthus* **sp.**
                                                (Animal-Flower)
Identification: The best field characters are the short, subby tenticles and the green-gray color of the individual members of the colony. *Size*: Individual's diameter about 0.5 inch (1.2 cm). *Habitat*: Found on shallow reefs. *Range*: Only reported from the Islas Revillagigedos.

7.   **BROWN ZOANTHID**   unidentified

Identification: These colonial anemones can be distinguished by their long brown tentacles and the sand covered column. *Size*: Height to 1 inch (2.5 cm). *Habitat*: Shallow reefs. *Range*: Upper Gulf of California.

8.   **SPOTTED ANEMONE**   *Antiparactis* **sp.**
                                              (Opposite; beside ray)
Identification: The best field characters are the brown spotting on the column and the bumps on the column are not in rows. The column also lacks a covering of sand and shell debris. *Size*: Width to about 3 inches (8 cm). *Habitat*: Shallow reefs. *Range*: Gulf of California.

9.   **ENCRUSTING STONY CORAL**   *Porites californica*
                                           (One who has pores; California)
Identification: The hard encrusting form and greenish color of this common genus of stony coral are the best field characters. Three different forms are illustrated; Form A and B were photographed in Bahia de Los Angeles, and Form C was photographed at Clarion Island. *Size*: Height to about 0.5 inches (1.3 cm). *Habitat*: Unpolluted, shallow, rocky reefs. *Range*: Gulf of California to Panama.

6. ZOANTHID ANEMONE

7. BROWN ZOANTHID

8. SPOTTED ANEMONE

9. ENCRUSTING STONY CORAL

10. BRANCHING STONY CORAL
Pocillopora elegans
(Little cup and pore; elegant)

Identification: The massive head, consisting of many thick branches with rounded ends and a very rough surface, is very distinctive. The color varies from brown to green. *Size*: Height to about 1.7 ft (0.5 m). *Habitat*: Shallow, unpolluted reefs. *Range*: Gulf of California; at least to Islas Revillagigedos.

11. COLONIAL CUP CORAL
Tubastraea, tenuilamellosa
(Starry tube; with thin small plates)

Identification: The bright yellow to orange color of the tentacles and the deep, circular shape of the individual cups (corallites) are good field identification characters. *Size*: Height to 11 inches (27.0 cm). *Habitat*: Occur usually on underside of rocks, and in crevices and caves; to depths of about 75 ft (23 m). *Range*: Gulf of California to Panama, including offshore islands.

12. BROWN CUP CORAL
Paracyathus sp.
(Next to cup)

Identification: These cup corals are distinguished by the brown color and the six to seven large septa, with many smaller septa in between. The diameter of the cup exceeds the height. *Size*: Diameter to about 0.75 inches (2 cm). *Habitat*: Shallow reefs. *Range*: Upper Gulf of California.

10. BRANCHING STONY CORAL

11. COLONIAL CUP CORAL

12. BROWN CUP CORAL

13. ROBUST GORGONIAN
Muricea sp.
(Purple one)

Identification: The best field characters for the genus are thick individual branches, usually at least twice as wide as the length of the individual polyps. The illustrations on the opposite page show: (a) A colony with white polyps, (b) Closeup of polyps, (c) Colony with yellow polyps; which is probably a different species, (d) Colony with purple branch and white polyps. *Size*: Colonies grow to heights of about 1.7 ft (51 cm). *Habitat*: Shallow offshore reefs to depths of about 100 ft (30 m). *Range*: Gulf of California to Panama.

14. BUMPY ORANGE GORGONIAN
Eugorgia aurantica
(True gorgon; orange colored)

Identification: The best field character is the very bumpy orange branches. The side branches are usually very short. *Size*: Height of colony to about 2.5 ft (0.8 m). *Habitat*: Offshore reefs and islands where these animals can find clean, plankton-rich water; to depths of about 100 ft (30 m). *Range*: Isla Cedros on outer coast and entire Gulf of California.

a

13. ROBUST GORGONIAN

b

c

R. Given

14. BUMPY ORANGE GORGONIAN

87

d

15. RED GORGONIAN

Eugorgia daniana

(True gorgon; after J. D. Dana)

Identification: This gorgonia is distinguished by the slender, red branches with white polyps. *Size*: Height to about 3 ft (0.9 m). *Habitat*: Offshore reefs and islands to depths of about 100 ft (30 m). *Range*: Central and lower Gulf of California.

16 YELLOW GORGONIAN

Eugorgia ampla

(True gorgon; large)

Identification: The best field characters are the yellow branches that, in some cases, are attached to their neighbor, forming a partial web. *Size*: Height to about 3 ft (0.9 m). *Habitat*: Offshore reefs and islands; to depths of about 100 ft (30 m). *Range*: Gulf of California.

17. WHITE GORGONIAN

Lophogorgia alba

(Tufted gorgon; white)

Identification: The long, slender white stalks lacking side branches are very distinctive. *Size*: Height to 3 ft (0.9 m). *Habitat*: Shallow reefs; to depths of 82 ft (25 m). *Range*: Gulf of California, common in Bahia de Los Angeles.

18. BROWN SEAFAN

Pacifigorgia sp.

(Pacific gorgonia)

Identification: The red, close-knit connecting branches with white polyps are good field characters. *Size*: Height to about 2.5 ft (0.8 m). *Habitat*: Offshore rocks and reefs to depths of at least 75 ft (23 m). *Range*: Central and lower Gulf of California.

15. RED GORGONIAN

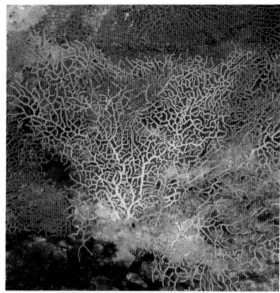

16. YELLOW GORGONIAN

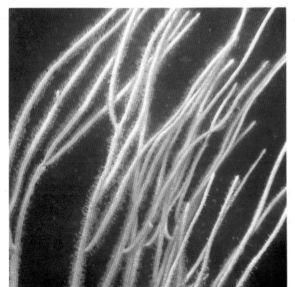

17. WHITE GORGONIAN

18. BROWN SEA FAN

19. YELLOW SEAFAN
Pacifigorgia sp.
(Pacific gorgonian)

Identification: The best field characters are the yellow, widely spaced, connecting branches with white polyps. *Size*: Height to about 2 ft (0.6 m). *Habitat*: Deep reefs and submarine canyons; to depths of at least 100 ft (30 m). *Range*: Lower Gulf of California.

20. RED SEAFAN
Gorgonia adamsi
(The gorgon medusa who had snakes for hair; Adam's)

Identification: The red, interconnected, widely spaced branches (spaces are about two branch widths wide) with white polyps are very distinctive. *Size*: Height to about 1 ft (30 cm). *Habitat*: Offshore reefs and rocks; to depths of about 120 ft (37 m). *Range*: Gulf of California.

21. YELLOW GORGONIAN
Filigella mitsukuri
(Small thread bearing one; Mitsukuri's)

Identification: The whitish stalks and yellow polyps are good field characters. *Size*: Height to about 1.3 ft (0.4 m). *Habitat*: Found on sand bottoms to depths of at least 100 ft (30 m). *Range*: San Benitos Islands. The southern range limit is unknown; not observed in the Gulf.

22. SEA PEN
Ptilosarcus undulatus
(Fleshy feather; wavy)

Identification: The best field characters are the large, fleshy lobes on the thick, central stalk. The color varies from translucent, light yellow to red-orange. *Size*: Height to about 1 ft (30 cm). *Habitat*: Muddy, sandy bottoms to depths of 65 ft (20 m). *Range*: Gulf of California.

19. YELLOW SEAFAN

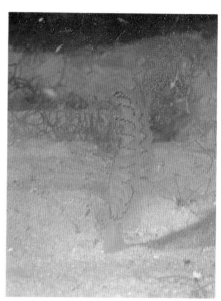

20. RED SEAFAN

21. GORGONIAN

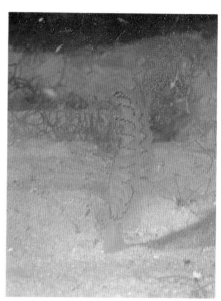

22. SEA PEN

PHYLUM ANNELIDA
Worms

23. GIANT SPIRALLED POLYCHAETE *Spirobranchus giganteus*
(Spiral gilt; gigantic)

Identification: The two spiralled feeding plumes are very distinctive. The color ranges from white to blue to red-orange. *Size*: Height of plumes to about 1 inch (2.5 cm). *Habitat*: Tubes are attached to coral heads and rocks; found to depths of about 50 ft (15 m). *Range*: Central and lower Gulf of California.

24. FEATHER DUSTER POLYCHAETE *Bispira* sp.
(Double-spiral)

Identification: The white and brown banded feeding plumes are the best field character. *Size*: Height about substrate to about 2 inches (5 cm). *Habitat*: Sand and gravel bottoms to depths of about 40 ft (12 m). *Range*: Gulf of California to Panama.

PHYLUM MOLLUSCA
Oysters, Scallops, Clams, Snails, Nudibranchs, Octopus, and Squid

25. SPINY OYSTER *Spondylus calcifer*
(Avertebra; bearing spurs)

Identification: The black and white banded fleshy mantle with yellow streaks is the best field character. *Size*: Diameter to about 6 inches (15 cm). *Habitat*: Occur on shallow rocks and reefs to depths of about 75 ft (23 m). *Range*: Gulf of California to Ecuador.

26. MUREX *Muricanthus princeps*
(Spined murex; first principal)

Identification: The spines and the brown-black and white bands are distinctive. *Size*: Length to about 5 inches (13 cm). *Habitat*: Shallow reefs to depths of about 75 ft (23 m). *Range*: Gulf of California to Peru.

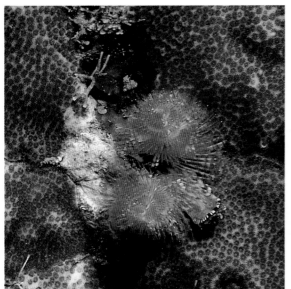

23. GIANT SPIRALLED POLYCHAETE

24. FEATHER DUSTER POLYCHAETE

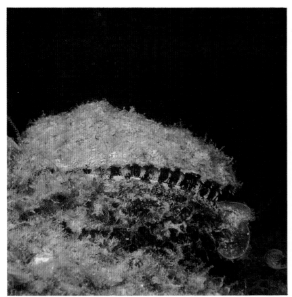

25. SPINY OYSTER

26. MUREX

27. GULF TULIP
Fasciolaria princeps
(Having little bands; first principal)

Identification: This snail, one of the largest in the Gulf, can be distinguished by the high spine and the orange to brown shell. The foot is orange or red with iridescent blue spots. *Size*: Length to 1 ft (30.5 cm). *Habitat*: Around shallow reefs on sand. *Range*: Gulf of California to Peru.

28. SPOTTED COWRY
Cypraea annettae
(Venus; woman's name)

Identification: The light blue shell with brown spots is a good field character. *Size*: Length to 1.5 inches (3.8 cm). *Habitat*: Shallow waters under rocks. *Range*: Outer coast of Baja California and throughout Gulf.

29. FRINGED ELYSID
Tridachiella diomeda
(Small one with three teeth; after Diomedes)

Identification: The best field character for this nudibranch is the colorful, fleshy frills on the back. *Size*: Length to 1.4 inches (3.6 cm). *Habitat*: Shallow reefs and rocks; to depths of about 50 ft (15 m). *Range*: Gulf of California to Panama.

30. NORRIS' DORID
Chromodoris norrisi
(Color sea goddess; Norris')

Identification: The purple and yellow dots on the white dorsal surface are distinctive. *Size*: Length to about 2.5 inches (6 cm). *Habitat*: Shallow rocks and algae. *Range*: Outer coast of Baja California, and Gulf of California.

31. RED TIPPED DORID
Chromodoris sedna
(Colorful sea goddess; Sedna's)

Identification: The best field characters are the white body with the red tipped gills and rhinophores (the paired fleshy sensory flaps on the head) and the yellow and red margins of the foot. *Size*: Length to 1.8 inches (4.6 cm). *Habitat*: Tidepools and rocky areas to depths of 65 ft (19.8 m). *Range*: Gulf of California to Nayarit, Mexico.

32. RED SPOTTED DORID
Chromodoris galexorum
(Colorful sea goddess; after Gale Sphon and Alex Kerstitch)

Identification: The large red spots with yellow borders are good field characters. *Size*: Length to about 1 inch (2.5 cm). *Habitat*: Shallow, rocky areas. *Range*: In the Gulf from Bahia de Los Angeles, south.

D. Behrens

27. GULF TULIP

28. SPOTTED COWRY

D. Behrens

29. FRINGED ELYSID

30. NORRIS' DORID

31. RED TIPPED DORID

32. RED SPOTTED DORID

95

33. OCTOPUS
Octopus sp.
(Eight legs)

Identification: There are at least nine species of octopus recorded from the Gulf. In most cases, it requires close in-hand examination to determine the species. The octopus illustrated is the common species I have observed in the waters around Islas Revillagigedos, and best fits the description of *O. hubbsorum*. *Size*: Length to about 2 ft (61 cm). *Habitat*: Shallow rocky and coral reefs. *Range*: Cabo San Lucas and Islas Revillagigedos.

PHYLUM ARTHROPODA
Shrimps, Lobsters, and Crabs

34. SOCORRO SPINY LOBSTER
Panulirus penicillatus
(Backward tail; a corruption of Palinurus = having tufts of fine hair, pencil-like)

Identification: The bright blue bases of the antenna are good field characters. *Size*: Weight to about 10 lb (4 kg). *Habitat*: Shallow rocky areas; to depths of about 75 ft (23 m). *Range*: Islas Revillagigedos, Tres Marias, Clipperton, and Galapagos on this coast. Also occurs off South Africa, in the Red Sea, and Indian Ocean.

35. BLUE SPINY LOBSTER
Panulirus inflatus
(Backward tail; inflated)

Identification: The orange spines on the front of the carapace and at the bases of the bluish antenna are distinctive. *Size*: Weight to about 8 lb (4 kg). *Habitat*: Shallow rocky areas. *Range*: Bahia Magdalena and Gulf of California to the Gulf of Tehuantepec.

36. CALIFORNIA SPINY LOBSTER
Panulirus interruptus
(Backward tail; broken, interrupted)

Identification: The general red coloration of the body is the best field character. *Size*: Length to over 2 ft (60 cm), and weight to 15 lb (7 kg). *Habitat*: Rocky areas to depths of 200 ft (61 m). *Range*: San Luis Obispo County, California to Magdalena Bay*, to Baja California and upper Gulf of California.

37. SLIPPER LOBSTER
Evibacus princeps
(With prominent welts; first principal)

Identification: The wide, flat body and lack of long antennae are good field characters. *Size*: Length to about 1.3 ft (0.4 cm). *Habitat*: Reefs with caves and crevices and sandy bottoms to depths of at least 100 ft (30 m). *Range*: Upper Gulf of California to Peru.

38. HERMIT CRAB
Aniculus elegans
(Small unconquerable one; elegant)

Identification: This large, hairy hermit crab can best be distinguished by the red bands on the legs and chelipeds (claws). *Size*: Length to about 6 inches (15 cm). *Habitat*: Rock, gravel, and coral heads; to depths of 80 ft (24 m). *Range*: Outer coast of Baja California, Gulf of California to Ecuador.

33. OCTOPUS

J. Dodd

34. SOCORRO SPINY LOBSTER

35. BLUE SPINY LOBSTER

36. CALIFORNIA SPINY LOBSTER

37. SLIPPER LOBSTER

38. HERMIT CRAB

PHYLUM ECHINODERMATA
Sea Stars, Brittle Stars, Urchins, Cucumbers

39. CROWN OF THORNS
Acanthaster ellisii
(Spine-star; Ellis')

Identification: The 10 to 15 short, spiny arms and the strongly pointed long and short spines on the upper body are very distinctive. *Size*: Diameter to about 1.5 ft (0.5 m). *Habitat*: Shallow reefs where there is an abundance of hard and soft corals; to depths of 80 ft (24 m). *Range*: Isla San Diego in Gulf to Peru.

40. SOCORRO CROWN OF THORNS
Acanthaster sp.
(Spine-star)

Identification: This sea star may or may not be a different species; they differ from the Gulf crown of thorns in the color pattern and they lack the small spines on the upper body. *Size*: Diameter to about 1.5 ft (0.5 m). *Habitat*: Shallow rock areas around corals. *Range*: Islas Revillagigedos.

41. GULF SUN STAR
Heliaster kubiniji
(Sun-star; Kubinijii's)

Identification: This many-armed star can be separated from the other Gulf sun star, *H. microbrachis*, by the presence of 19 to 25 arms (rays) as compared with the 30 to 40 arms of *H. microbrachius*. *Size*: Diameter to about 2 ft (0.6 m). *Habitat*: Shallow reefs and sand bottoms. *Range*: Gulf of California to Nicaragua.

42. FRAGILE STAR
Linckia columbiae
(Lincks'; dove)

Identification: The best field characters are the gray and red mottling, arms of unequal length, and the nearly round cross section of the arms. *Size*: Diameter to about 6 inches (15 cm). *Habitat*: Shallow rocky areas; to depths of about 24 ft (7.3 m). *Range*: San Pedro, California, and the upper Gulf of California to Peru.

39. CROWN OF THORNS

40. SOCORRO CROWN OF THORNS

41. GULF SUNSTAR

42. FRAGILE STAR

43. PURPLE STAR
Linckia sp.
(Lincks')

Identification: The almost round arms and the dark purple coloration are distinctive. *Size*: Diameter to about 6 inches (15 cm). *Habitat*: Shallow reefs and sandy bottoms. *Range*: Only observed in the central Gulf, but it probably ranges south of the Gulf.

44. RED SPOTTED STAR
Linckia sp.
(Lincks')

Identification: The red spots on a gray background of this *Linckia* are distinctive. *Size*: Diameter to about 1 ft (30 cm). *Habitat*: Rocky and coral reefs. *Range*: Observed only at Clarion Island; it may be the same species as that occuring in Hawaii (*L. multifora*).

45. YELLOW SPOTTED STAR
Pharia pyramidata
(Lighthouse-like; pyramid-shaped)

Identification: The large yellow to orange spots on the arms are the best field character. *Size*: Diameter to about 1 ft (30 cm). *Habitat*: Shallow rocks and reefs to depths of about 50 ft (15 m). *Range*: Gulf of California to Peru, including the Galapagos Islands.

46. TAN STAR
Phataria unifascialis
(Resembling *Pharia*; with single bundles)

Identification: This star resembles the yellow spotted star, except that the color pattern is tan with two orange stripes on each arm. *Size*: Diameter to about 1 ft (30 cm). *Habitat*: Shallow rocks and reefs; to depths of about 60 ft (18 m). *Range*: Bahia de Los Angeles in upper Gulf to Peru, including the Galapagos Islands.

43. PURPLE STAR

44. RED SPOTTED STAR

45. YELLOW SPOTTED STAR

46. TAN STAR

47. ORANGE STAR

Othilia tenuispina
(Thrusting; thin spine)

Identification: The color pattern of yellow-brown to orange or red and the dark red to black spot on the tip of each arm is distinctive. *Size*: Diameter to about 4 inches (10 cm). *Habitat*: Shallow rocks and reefs. *Range*: Gulf of California, common only in upper Gulf.

48. CHOCOLATE CHIP STAR

Nidorellia armata
(Small reeking one; armed)

Identification: The short, thick arms and color pattern of black spots on the cream colored upper body are very distinctive. *Size*: Diameter to about 5 inches (13 cm). *Habitat*: Shallow reefs. *Range*: Gulf of California to Peru.

49. GULF STAR

Oreaster occidentalis
(Mountain-star: western)

Identification: The robust arms covered with bright red spines are very distinctive. *Size*: Diameter to about 6 inches (15 cm). *Habitat*: Shallow reefs and sand bottoms to depths of about 60 ft (18 m). *Range*: Gulf of California to Peru, including the Galapagos Islands. This is the most abundant star at scuba depths in the central and lower Gulf.

50. SPINY STAR

Amphiaster insignis
(Double-star; well-marked)

Identification: The best field characters are the long, robust spines on the red arms and body. *Size*: Diameter to about 4 inches (10 cm). *Habitat*: Shallow reefs. *Range*: Central Gulf of California to Panama; uncommon.

47. ORANGE STAR

48. CHOCOLATE CHIP STAR

49. GULF STAR

50. SPINY STAR

51. SEA STAR   *Mithrodia bradleyi*
(Like a Persian precious stone; Bradley's)
Identification: The long slender arms covered with short spines and the red and brown color are good field characters. *Size*: Diameter to about 8 inches (20 cm). *Habitat*: Shallow reefs to depths of about 80 ft (24 m). *Range*: Central Gulf to Panama, including Islas Revillagigedos and Galapagos.

52. BRITTLE STAR   *Ophionereis occidentalis*
(Serpent worm; western)
Identification: The black and white banded, long, slender, spiny arms are distinctive. *Size*: Diameter to about 8 inches (20 cm). *Habitat*: Shallow reefs, usually under rocks or in crevices. *Range*: Gulf of California to Ecuador, including the Galapagos Islands.

53. BASKET STAR   *Astrodictyum panamense*
(Star-net; associated with Panama)
Identification: The best field characters are the many branched, brown banded arms. *Size*: Length of extended arms to about 1 ft (30 cm). *Habitat*: Found attached to gorgonians in shallow water. *Range*: Gulf of California.

55. SEA URCHIN   *Arbacia incisa*
(After Arbakes, first king of Media in Greek mythology; cut into)
Identification: The dark color and lateral spines that are slightly longer than the diameter of the test are good field characters. *Size*: Diameter to about 3 inches (8 cm). *Habitat*: Shallow reefs and rocks. *Range*: Gulf of California to Peru, including the Galapagos Islands.

51. SEA STAR

52. BRITTLE STAR

54. BASKET STAR

54. SEA URCHIN

55. SLATE PENCIL URCHIN
Eucidaris thouarsii
(True turban; Thouar's)

Identification: The thick, blunt-tipped, pencil-like spines are very distinctive. *Size*: Diameter to about 7 inches (18 cm). *Habitat*: Found in crevices on shallow reefs; to depths of about 500 ft (152 m). *Range*: Santa Catalina Island, California, and the Gulf of California to Ecuador, including the offshore islands.

56. FLOWER URCHIN
Toxopneustes roseus
(Bow, breathing; rose-colored)

Identification: The very short spines and long, petal shaped pedicellariae give this urchin a distinctive flower appearance. *Size*: Diameter to about 5 inches (13 cm). *Habitat*: Shallow reefs. *Range*: Central Gulf to Ecuador, including offshore islands.

57. BROWN URCHIN
Tripneustes depressus
(Three, breathing; depressed)

Identification: The abundant, short spines and large test are very distinctive. *Size*: Diameter to about 7 inches (18 cm). *Habitat*: Shallow reefs. *Range*: La Pas to Galapagos Islands, including Islas Revillagigedos.

58. CROWNED URCHIN
Centrostephanus coronatus
(Crowned with spines, crowned)

Identification: The very long, slender, serrated spines and dark purple color are good field characters. The Coranado sea urchin resembles the toxic urchin, *Diadema mexicanum* (NI), but the latter species have long, smooth, white and purple banded spines. *Size*: Diameter to about 6 inches (15 cm); spines about twice as long as diameter of test. *Habitat*: Shallow reefs, in crevices; to depths of about 350 ft (107 m). *Range*: Channel Islands, California, and Gulf of Ecuador, and the offshore islands.

55. SLATE PENCIL URCHIN

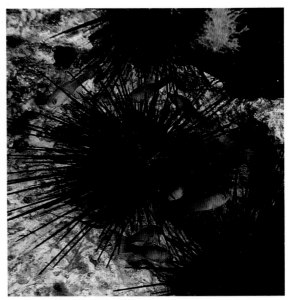

56. FLOWER URCHIN

57. BROWN URCHIN

58. CROWNED URCHIN

59. CUCUMBER — *Holothuria zacae*

(A kind of zoophyte; after zaca)

Identification: The best field characters are the many short papillae on the dark gray body with only a few large papillae. *Size*: Length to about 1 ft (30 cm). *Habitat*: Shallow reefs and sand and mud bottoms. *Range*: Santa Catalina Island, California, and the Gulf of California to the Galapagos Islands.

60. BROWN CUCUMBER — *Holothuria inhabilis*

(A kind of zoophyte; inhabiting)

Identification: The flat, ridged, brown body with stubby papillae is distinctive. *Size*: Length to 1 ft (30 cm). *Habitat*: Found on sandy or mud bottoms and occasionally on reefs; to depths of about 80 ft (24 m). *Range*: Bahia Concepcion and Gulf of California to Costa Rica; including offshore islands.

61. BROWN SPOTTED CUCUMBER — *Brandtothuria impatiens*

(Brandt's zoophyte; unable to endure)

Identification: The brown spotted body covered with many black-tipped papillae is distinctive. *Size*: Length to about 6 inches (15 cm). *Habitat*: Shallow sandy and mud bottoms and rocky areas. *Range*: Gulf of California to Columbia, and the Galapagos Islands.

62. SYNAPTED CUCUMBER — *Euapta godeffroyi*

(Well-fastened; Godeffroy's)

Identification: The best field characters are the long, soft, snake-like body that lacks tube feet, and the long feather-like feeding tentacles. *Size*: Length when fully extended to at least 3 ft (0.9 m). *Habitat*: These snake-like cucumbers come out to feed at night on and around shallow rocks and reefs. *Range*: Tropical Indo-Pacific; on this coast from the central Gulf to Panama.

59. CUCUMBER

60. BROWN CUCUMBER

61. BROWN SPOTTED CUCUMBER

62. SYNAPTED CUCUMBER

BIBLIOGRAPHY

Behrens, D. W. 1980. *Pacific Coast Nudibranchs, A Guide to the Opisthobranchs of the Northeastern Pacific.* Sea Challengers, Los Osos, California. 112 p.

Brusca, R. C. 1980. *Common Intertidal Invertebrates of the Gulf of California.* University of Arizon Press, Tucson, Arizona. 513 p.

Farley, M. B., and L. K. Farley. 1978. *Diving Mexico's Baja California.* Marcor Enterprises, Port Hueneme, California. 176 p.

Gotshall, D. W. 1981. *Pacific Coast Inshore Fishes.* Sea Challengers, Los Osos, California. 96 p.

Gotshall, D. W., and L. L. Laurent. 1979 *Pacific Coast Subtidal Marine Invertebrates.* Sea Challengers, Los Osos, California. 112 p.

Hobson, E. S. 1968. Predatory behavior of some shore fishes in the Gulf of California. U.S. Fish and Wildlife Service Research Department. (73): 92 p.

Miller, D. W. and R. N. Lea. 1976. Guide to the Coastal Marine Fishes of California. California Department of Fish and Game, Fish Bulletin (157): 1-249.

Keen, M. A. 1971. *Sea Shells of Tropical West America, from Baja California to Peru.* Second Edition. Stanford University Press, Stanford, California. 626 p.

Morris. R. H., D. P. Abbott, and E. C. Haderlie. 1980. *Intertidal Invertebrates of California.* Stanford University Press, Stanford, California. 690 p.

Randall, J. E. 1982. *Underwater Guide to Hawaiian Reef Fishes.* Harrowood Books, Newtown Square, Pennsylvania. 72 p.

Sainz, J. C. 1976. *Catalogo de Peces Marinos Mexicanos.* Instituto Nacional le Pesta, Mexico D. F. 462 p.

Thomson, D. A., L. T Findley, and A. N. Kerstitch. 1979. *Reef Fishes of the Sea of Cortez.* John Wiley and Sons, New York, New York. 302 p.

Thomson, D. A., and W. McKibbin. 1976. *Gulf of California Fishwatchers Guide.* Golden Puffer Press, Tucson, Arizona. 75 p.

Walford, L. A. 1974. *Marine Game Fishes of the Pacific Coast from Alaska to the Equator.* Smithsonian Instituion Reprint by T. F. H. Publications, Inc., Neptune, New Jersey. 205 p. 70 plates.

INDEX